DARE TO DREAM

DARE TO DREAM

Connecticut Basketball's
Remarkable March
to the
National
Championship

JIM CALHOUN

with

Leigh Montville

Broadway Books
New York

To the memory of Joe McGinn.

To all of my players, past and present,
who have made my basketball life a wonderful journey.

To all of my assistant coaches, laboring long and hard
as we collectively pursue excellence.

Most important, to my family.

To my wife, Pat.

To my sons, Jim and Jeff.

To my daughter-in-law, Jen and
my future daughter-in-law, Amy.

And to my granddaughter, Emily.

Published in the United States by Broadway Books, an imprint of
The Doubleday Publishing Group, a division of Random House, Inc., New York.
www.broadwaybooks.com

A hardcover edition of this book was published in 1999 by Broadway Books.

BROADWAY BOOKS and its logo, a letter B bisected on the diagonal,
are trademarks of Random House, Inc.

www.broadwaybooks.com

Book design by Tina Thompson
Original Jacket Design by Andrea Thomas
Jacket Photographs by © Bob Stowell (Front), David Gonzales/NCAA Photos (Back)

Cataloging-in-Publication Data for the hardcover is on file with the Library of Congress.

Hardcover Edition ISBN: 978-0-7679-2954-3
Trade Paperback ISBN: 978-0-7679-2954-7

146866421

Contents

Prologue

You think you know what you're doing. That's the thing. You work every day, every year, hard as you can. You think sometimes—even in a business where your face is on the television screen, your name is in the newspaper, and the results of your work are printed in agate type in the standings—that you're all alone.

You have no idea how many people are paying attention. No idea . . .

Dear Coach Calhoun,

After many happy years together, both of my parents passed away this past year; my father on Nov. 23, my mother just this past Mar. 17. My Dad, whom I always was very close to, went to a rehab/nursing home in September after having a small stroke, pneumonia, and some other problems. After thinking he'd recover fully, he developed more health problems and slowly began to go. My Dad, like you, was a Boston native, lived in Dedham, then relocated to Connecticut in the '50s. He loved the Huskies and always talked about the games. [He passed away] and then my mother died of a sudden, unexpected heart attack. It was a shock to our family.

I can't explain how depressed I was at her death. I was in

shock and in pain that few can understand. The night of her funeral, my husband and I watched your game in Arizona and he said, "We're going to St. Petersburg." Not being sure I really could do it, in the haze of pain I was in, I gradually agreed to go. We DROVE DOWN NON-STOP with two other people. Despite the sheer exhaustion and hunger, it was all worthwhile because of you and your team.

I want to thank you FROM THE BOTTOM OF MY HEART for putting a smile on my face and happy tears in my eyes. You don't know how much your hardworking, determined, gutsy team has meant to myself and others in similar circumstances. Your victory is our victory. We love you all and thank you—please extend to the team the fact that we love and appreciate them more than they know and how their win is somehow all our win, especially for those facing tough times.

Joan Sheehan
Glastonbury, CT

You are caught up with the mundane, the small emergencies of the moment that never end. There always is another call to make, another kid to see, another meeting, another 20-second time-out to take to discuss the problem that suddenly has arisen. . . .

Dear Coach Calhoun and Team,

I'm a UConn graduate, Class of '52, and I've seen a lot of games, from Vinny Yokabaskas down through the years to the TV thrills of Scott Burrell's fantastic toss to Tate George for his last-second basket, and for all the wonderful moments of

Donyell Marshall, Donny Marshall, "The Dove," and Ray Allen, to mention a few. . . .

Yesterday I bought a basketball, blue and white, with Jonathan [the UConn mascot] and the words "UConn Huskies" on it. . . . I raised the UConn banner on my flagpole and donned one of my two lucky UConn sweatshirts. (I change at halftime.) With the basketball at my feet, dressed in "full battle array," I watched with clenched, sweaty palms until those last few glorious seconds when I realized you didn't need MY help, you were doing just fine! After the game, I opened my front door and let out a war whoop that, if it didn't wake all the neighbors, at least frightened a few deer out of the yard!

Thank you, thank you. You made an old lady happy!!

Natalie Hermandorfer
Easton, CT

You have no idea . . .

Dear UConn,

I think you are a good team. You have good defense and offense. I like to watch your games. I taped the game against Duke. I'm glad you won! Ricky Moore had some nice shots. I liked when Khalid had three men on him and still got the shot. My family wanted UConn to win! My teacher, Mr. Theroux, likes UConn, too! He wrote "UConn National Champions" on the board.

Michael Bhatt
Cromwell, CT

No idea at all . . .

Dear Jim,

We are UConn Alumni, classmates of '53, and have been going to UConn basketball games since we first met in Storrs in 1951. Storrs is sacred ground to us. It's where we met and ultimately celebrated our engagement a few days before we graduated together forty-six years ago. We're season ticket holders for [the men's and women's teams] and have been for many years. You have brought a special joy to our lives since you arrived some years ago and we want to thank you for that and congratulate you on your NCAA championship.

We volunteer at the Grey Cancer Center at Hartford Hospital on Friday mornings. Last Friday, a woman who appeared to be well into her nineties arrived for chemotherapy treatment wearing a UConn championship T-shirt. Norton said to her, "How about those Huskies?" She lit up, eyes wide with a huge grin, and proudly responded, "You know, I stayed up till 11:30 and saw the whole damned game and loved every minute of it."

We thought you should have yet another example of how your good work brings happiness to so many.

Janice and Norton Glass
Avon, CT

You are caught in that dark tunnel of work. Everybody is. You are just doing what you're supposed to do . . .

Dear Coach Calhoun,

I am a 1973 UConn graduate. I recently lost my husband to brain cancer. I am pleased to say that during his illness, from Dec. 5, 1997, to Dec. 1998, he always felt well enough to watch every game, never missing any. He asked for a TV in neuro intensive care before and after his surgery.

Your team, your wonderful group of talented and friendly and generally pleasant guys, is what got my entire family through our worst nightmare and tragedy. Whenever I watched a game, I could forget my own misery and completely immerse myself in total Huskymania. When we got past that locked door [into the Final Four] this year was great, but almost even better was kicking Duke's butt.... Before my husband passed away, I whispered in his ear at Connecticut Hospice, "Lee, when you get to Heaven, make sure the Huskies win."

Now he knows he's made it.

Susan Mohn
North Haven, CT

You come out of the tunnel.

You are amazed by the brightness of the light.

Chapter 1

FINAL FOUR

Dear Jim,

What a great time for you, the team and your family. Your new little granddaughter, Emily, is precious (I saw you hold her picture for the camera when you were being interviewed).

I have started this letter to you before the game begins— just to tell you how proud I am and feel. I have a very strong feeling that your old coach is looking down on you and smiling with great pride. He would be so happy for you.

I have the newspapers from around this area. You really have put old Braintree in the headlines. I can empathize with Pat and all of your family for all the pressures you are going through, but you'll handle it to perfection . . .

Mrs. Fred Herget
Braintree, MA

I was down to my last dress shirt, and it was not a great shirt. I guess that is what happens when you never have been to the final game of the Final Four. You simply don't know how to pack. Other things seem more important.

The sleeves on the shirt were about an inch too short. The collar on the shirt simply wouldn't settle, the white wings on either side of my tie looking like they had started to fly out the windows of the suite at the Hyatt Regency Westshore in Tampa and into the Florida sky. I was not a picture from *Gentlemen's Quarterly.*

"You don't have something else?" my wife, Pat, asked as I finished dressing.

"It's all that was left in the bag," I replied.

There was no debate about the tie. It was the same patterned purple tie I'd worn nine days earlier at the America West Arena in Phoenix, Arizona. It was a match for the black suit I'd also worn at the America West Arena. A friend, Bill Mitchell, a clothier in Westport, Connecticut, had given me three suits to wear for the weekend, but I was sticking with what I knew.

Pat was worried that the suit might have shrunk from the water dumped on top of me at the end of that Arizona afternoon—University of Connecticut 67, Gonzaga 62—but apparently it had come back from the cleaners in fine shape. If it had shrunk, well, it would match the shirt, then, wouldn't it?

This was not a time for great changes.

·   ·   ·

I was the lead character in the story—not a story, really, but a saga—that was going to be played into the Neilsen-rated homes of America on this night of March 29, 1999. The Coach Who Couldn't Get to the Final Four. That was me. Now not only was I at the Final Four, I had a shot to win the damn thing. A 9½-point underdog's shot, perhaps, but a shot.

The University of Connecticut vs. Duke.

NCAA Championship Game. 9:18 P.M. (EST)

The Tropicana Dome, St. Petersburg, FL

CBS (Jim Nantz and Billy Packer).

I was cast as the coaching veteran of 27 years, the new grandfather, 56 years old, who had shown the patience of Job, the perseverance of Sisyphus, pushing that boulder up that long, torturous hill. I had reached the summit at last. The chains were gone; the great cloud had lifted.

I, to tell the truth, was less charmed by the tale than just about anyone. I gave no time to it. None at all.

I simply wanted to win that damn game.

 ●   ●   ●

The question had been coming at me for almost ten years now. Yes? The stocky gentleman in the back of the room with the notebook and the mustard stain on his shirt? Yes? How do I feel about not going to the Final Four? Well . . .

I always had refused to be judged by whether or not my teams from UConn advanced those last couple of steps. Would I have been a better coach if the shot by Duke's Christian Laettner had rimmed out or fallen short in 1990 . . . if Donyell Marshall, our best foul shooter, had made one of two against Florida in 1994 . . . if we hadn't been sent to play UCLA in 1995 in California, or North Carolina in 1998 in North Carolina . . . if and if and if? Nonsense.

That litany of doom had grown longer and longer with the end of each season, but I never changed my explanation. The NCAA tournament was a tightrope, understand? One subtle push, one unforeseen rush of air, and you can be sitting at home with your mending clavicle, your surgically repaired pelvis. Your broken heart. Anything can happen in a single-elimination tournament. Excellence was climbing back on that tightrope, again and again. Excellence was inching forward, step by step. Excellence was a long-term proposition. I didn't feel any differently now.

"It's great you've finally made it after all you've been through," people would say, meaning well.

"Thank you" was the answer I gave. But what I wanted to say was, "What do you mean, 'after all I've been through'? Do you mean six Big East championships in the nineties, five in the last six years? Do you mean seven trips to the Sweet Sixteen in the past 10 years? Do you mean the four 30-win seasons, an average of 26 wins every year in the past decade? Yeah, it's a bitch. I make over $500,000 every year, my physical health is fine, and my mental health, while always questionable, at least seems to stay the same. Yeah, I've been through a lot."

I was the same coach I always had been, the same guy. I had the same values, same ideas. The perception that I was better, that I somehow had changed, that I had done something differently this time was ridiculous. The package might have changed—different styles for the nineties than the seventies—but the contents were the same. I was the same guy who had watched Laettner's shot go through the basket at the buzzer, making it Duke 79, UConn 78 in overtime. Maybe a little older, but probably not much wiser.

"This Is Our Time" was the message I had written on the blackboard again and again during our long season.

Maybe it was as simple as that. Maybe this *was* our time.

Maybe not.

I would still be the same coach I always had been.

• • •

The University of Connecticut might never have been to another Final Four, but it had been at this one forever. I had brought the team into

Tampa on Wednesday night, a day before Duke and Michigan State and Ohio State arrived. It was silly, I suppose, a little bit of gamesmanship that probably meant nothing, but I liked the idea that we were already there on Thursday morning, when the other teams were just getting ready to make the trip. On my personal scoreboard, that gave us the early lead. It let us establish our patterns, our routines, first.

I am a believer in routines.

I like familiarity.

I had talked with a few coaches who had taken teams to other Final Fours. There are different strategies about whether to let the kids go, let them enjoy the event, or to hold the reins in a tight grip and be all business. I probably chose a path somewhere in the middle, but I did have hold of those reins. No doubt about that.

I picked the Hyatt Westshore, near the Tampa airport, from a list of hotels offered by the NCAA. I liked the idea that it largely had been booked by CBS, so it wouldn't be filled with fans. I liked the idea that it was away from the action downtown. It had two pools, the second one hidden and private. I liked the two pools.

The first thing we do on any road trip, even a bus ride to Boston College for an overnight, is meet in the captain's room (we had co-captains, Ricky Moore and Rashamel Jones, but mostly always we met in Ricky's room). I like the way everyone is crowded together. I can see all the eyes.

I start by laying out the schedule for the rest of the night and the next day: up at 7:30, breakfast at 8:30, bus for practice at 9:30, practice at 10 . . . it's all out there, bang, bang, bang. I then deliver a message of some kind.

"You're going to really enjoy this week, but the reason we're here is to win a national championship," was this message. "Every team here—Duke, of course, and Michigan State, Ohio State—is on a roll. But the opponent doesn't make any difference. We're here to win a national championship."

The hotel becomes your home pretty quickly. The arena becomes your place of work. The 30-minute trip from hotel to arena—in this case on a long causeway between Tampa and St. Petersburg—becomes your commute. By the sixth day, when the championship game arrived for us, we couldn't have been more settled if we had a second mortgage and crabgrass.

Example 1: On Friday night we ate a team dinner in the hotel dining room. It was a terrific restaurant, good food, but too good for the kids, if you know what I mean. When the chicken cordon bleu arrived, they all looked at it as if it were food for aliens. Most of the team went out for fast-food replacements as soon as the meal was done.

On Sunday night we ate again at the restaurant. We thought about taking the kids somewhere else, but decided against it because we wanted to conserve all energies for Monday. We did talk to the restaurant about the menu, though, and this time the chicken was fried, brought in from outside with burgers and fries and hot dogs. Everybody loved it.

Example 2: Probably the moment it hit me first and best that we were playing for the national championship came on Sunday, when we went to practice at Tropicana Field. The dressing rooms for Ohio State and Michigan State were now empty. The little signs with the names were still on the doors, but the people were gone. Duke and Connecticut were the only ones left.

"You can switch to the Michigan State room if you'd like," an NCAA official said. "It might be a better room."

"Noooo," I said. "We'll just stay where we are."

Familiarity.

·   ·   ·

The plotting and planning for Duke mostly had taken place in my suite on Saturday night—the early hours of Sunday, really. After we beat Ohio State, 64–58, in our half of the semifinal doubleheader, my coaches and I stayed around to watch Duke outlast Michigan State, 68–62, in the second game. We then went back to the hotel, celebrated a little bit, ate dinner with our families, but gathered in my room at midnight.

In our first practice in Florida, at Hillsborough Community College on Thursday, we'd worked on some of the things that we had to do for

Duke. It was a generic practice, really, but there was a definite Duke tinge to it. I know it sounds cart-before-the-horse crazy, working on Duke before we played Ohio State, but it was our last chance for a hard workout. We could put the Ohio State stuff in the next day. By this point in the season, we'd had 123, 124 practices, including game days, and we had the basics down pretty well. It was okay to work a bit on Duke.

We practiced a big-man double team we'd need to contain Elton Brand, Duke's large-bodied center, the college player of the year. We worked on a little bit of zone defense that maybe we'd need if the double team didn't work. We refined our perimeter defense, which we'd need against Duke, but also would need against Ohio State or Michigan State.

I also had my blue index cards, which later would become borderline famous. During the season, watching a game at home, I'd make notes to myself on things I saw Duke do. It was nothing out of the ordinary. I like to watch games. I'm the guy in your office who'll say, "Hey, did you see that Pepperdine–Santa Clara game last night?" (You'll say, "Didn't that game start at midnight?") I'll jot down things other coaches do, ways they'll run a certain offense differently from the way we do, looking to see if I can improve the way we do things.

I'd made a bunch of notes on Duke mostly because Duke was on television a lot. I probably made more notes on Temple, to tell the truth, because I always had a feeling we were going to run into Temple, with its tough zone defense, somewhere along the way. This never happened, so the blue cards for Temple stayed on my desk. The blue cards for Duke came to the Final Four.

I liked our chances; that was my first thought. I liked our chances a lot.

I suppose the oddsmakers and the media were swayed, rightfully so, by the fact Duke had won 32 straight games and had 7 McDonald's All-Americans on the roster, a staggering collection of high-school talent coached by Mike Krzyzewski, only the most successful coach of our generation. I suppose they questioned us because we had only two McDonald's All-Americans—Richard Hamilton and Khalid El-Amin—and we'd lost twice in the second half of the season. We certainly weren't as convincing in our wins as Duke was; in fact, we'd trailed at halftime in nine games we'd won.

I thought everyone was missing a few things. No. 1, we had more experience. Duke, with all that talent, was still a very young team. Corey Maggette, the great kid off the bench, certain NBA player, was a freshman. Good as he might be, he still would make freshman mistakes. No. 2, we had more speed. We lost on size on most indvidual matchups, but we made up for it with speed. No. 3, we might have lost two games during the season, but in neither one of them were we whole, healthy. We were whole, healthy now. The nine games in which we trailed at halftime? I thought the fact that we had the grit, the resolve, to come back nine times was more important than the fact that we had trailed nine times.

I liked the way we played together as a unit. Cohesiveness seems to be a rare quality these days. The teams I watched as a kid—the Boston Celtics, winning all those championships with Cousy and Russell, Heinsohn and Sam and K. C. Jones—were based on unselfishness, on roles, on everyone doing his own job. Who scored the points never mattered. Which team won the game did. That was how our team played.

Richard Hamilton—6'6", 185 pounds—the scorer.

Khalid El-Amin—5'10", 203 pounds—the point guard, the motor that keeps the whole operation running.

Ricky Moore—6'2", 195 pounds—the defender.

Kevin Freeman—6'7", 235 pounds—the constant, the janitor under the glass.

Jake Voskuhl—6'11", 245 pounds—the goalie, the last line of defense.

Put this unit against, say, those Kentucky teams of a few years ago. You'd look at Kentucky, with seven future pros—guys like Antoine Walker, Ron Mercer, Jamal Mashburn, and the rest—and you'd say the talent matchup was ridiculous. You'd be right. But you know what? Play a game of basketball, five against five, and I think we'd win the game. I really think so.

I also thought we'd win the game against Duke.

*   *   *

9

I was late to the Blue Devils' victory over Michigan State in the semis, held up by the postgame interviews and hoo-ha after Ohio State, but one thing was obvious as I watched the second half: Duke was not the same team when Elton Brand was not involved. The big man had three fouls and sat for a while. That was when Michigan State came back. The big man returned. That was when Michigan State died.

Our first job was to try to take Elton out of the game. Our obvious strategy was to double-team him with our two big men, Kevin and Jake. Every time he got the ball, Kevin and Jake would converge on him and our other three players would try to fill the hole created in the rest of our defense. This was nothing new. Kevin and Jake had been playing the big-man double for three years now, playing it against every good big man we met.

"Michigan State tried it," Tom Moore, my assistant, said, "but Michigan State doesn't have the defensive speed we have. It's interesting, our defensive speed. It somehow doesn't translate on film. Teams look at us, but they don't get a feel for how fast we really are. They always are surprised by it."

The second thing we had to do was to get the ball out of point guard William Avery's hands. I felt he was the one ball handler Duke had, the Blue Devil's version of Khalid. We had to pressure him, force him to pass to someone else. Maybe we could put Ricky on him, at least at the start. We wanted Trajan Langdon, the other guard, the shooter, to do the bulk of the ball handling, but we also had to get someone on him on the outside, not let him shoot the three-pointer.

Our third problem was pace. I was convinced we didn't want to get involved in an up-and-down shootout with Duke. If that happened, if the score were 96–90, we would lose. Duke averaged 10 points per game more than we did. There was a reason for that. Duke had better offensive players than we did. We had to play under control on offense a little bit, which sometimes was hard for us to do, especially with Khalid running the show, but we had to do it here.

There were some other things Tom and Dave Leitao and Karl Hobbs and I discussed, but these were the important ones. This was the blueprint. We ate bad food—pass the french fries—and talked until four in the morning. Not bad for us. We imparted the message to the team the next day.

With passion.

．　．　．

"You can create, in two hours, a lifetime of memories," I told the team. "You've had a great season, 33–2, and I'll be proud of you no matter what, but in this one game you have a chance to do something that is very special. And there is no doubt in my mind you can do that."

I told them this again and again. Our time.

At the Sunday practice, scheduled for an hour and a half, with maybe three hours of needed work laid out in my head, I pulled the plug after about 50 minutes. I looked around Tropicana Field at all those empty seats; looked at the kids; thought about the practice, which had been pretty good but nothing special; and decided enough was enough. I very rarely do that. The kids looked at me. Maybe I *was* a tad dramatic about it.

"You're ready," I said. "The things that we are, we aren't going to be able to change. The things that Duke is, they aren't going to be able to change. The quickness of our feet and our ability to take away their strengths is only going to get better, and there's nothing they can do about it. And it's going to be . . ."

Our time.

In the team meeting at the hotel on Sunday night, I played on our role as the underdog. I always have loved being the underdog. Throughout my coaching career, my teams have had some great underdog games. It is so much easier being the underdog, with the world against you, something to prove. I fret the worst during the season before the games we are supposed to win easily—the game against Quinnipiac, which we're supposed to capture in a romp. What if our kids aren't motivated? What if their kids somehow explode? Ask anyone, I am most anxious before the game where we are supposed to cruise.

As we have become better and better through the years, there have been fewer and fewer chances to be the underdog. I now often have to fuel that underdog fire synthetically. I listen to the airheads on sports radio talk shows. That always can get me going. I read. I read anything, everything. Write something bad—even a little bit bad—about our team in the *Waterbury Republican* or the *New Haven Register* or the Yakima, Washington, *Bugle,* and I will see it and respond. They say we can't do this? Can't do that? I eat this stuff like M&Ms, like vitamin pills.

There was no shortage of M&Ms now.

"Confidence is not a problem for Connecticut, not like, oh, inside defense, shot selection, or, judging by the waistline of its star point guard, Khalid El-Amin, second helpings of everything," Bernie Lincicome of the *Chicago Tribune* wrote. "A team so flawed as this ought not be so full of itself, though it is certainly full of something. . . . UConn has had its nose pressed up against the window [of the Final Four] so long it looks like a decal."

Okay, Bernie.

"Brand might foul out 6'11" Jake Voskuhl in warm-ups," Skip Bayless, also of the *Tribune,* wrote. "All those thuggish Huskies will look like Lilliputians against a sophomore from Peekskill, N.Y."

Right, Skip.

Tom Moore does our scouting reports. He is a young guy, energetic, talented, organized. He watches more tape of more teams than anyone I know. I sort of blindsided him. Sorry, Tom.

He ran about 11 minutes of breakdown tape on Duke at our Sunday meeting. There was stuff on offense, stuff on defense, then stuff on maybe their top 8 or 9 individual players. It was the usual nuts and bolts, about how "Elton likes to get the ball on the left block and then turn back to find the open man," and so on. One player after another. Avery does this. Langdon does that.

As he talked, Tom also delivered some opinons. He said Avery might be the best point guard we faced all year. He said Langdon might be the best shooter we faced. Elton might be the best player we faced. I could hear some of the kids moaning about this. When Tom got to backup forward Chris Burgess and said, "He might be the best defensive forward we've faced," I could hear someone, I think it was Kevin, say, "Yeah, right." There were some giggles.

I took the floor after Tom. I lambasted him.

"Apparently the 1,600 writers here, the oddsmakers, think Duke is 10 to 12 points better than us," I said. "And even *our assistant coach* thinks they're a hell of a team. Everybody thinks Duke's great—and it has been, for 32 straight games. But do you know what? In those 32 games, Duke hasn't faced the University of Connecticut.

"They don't know about your character. They don't know about your quickness. Well, in less than 24 hours they're going to know. You're going to beat Duke. I'm not saying Duke isn't good. They are as good as you. But there are things we can do against them, and there isn't anything they can do against you. There's nothing they can do in that hotel room tonight that's going to put foot speed on Elton, on Shane Battier, on Burgess . . ."

It kind of went on from there.

I said once during the season that I've always seen myself as a Don Quixote kind of guy, charging off at impossible causes, windmills. My wife disagreed. She said I was smarter than Don Quixote, that my causes always had substance, that my windmills need to be attacked.

I don't know about that. I do know it felt good to be back in the saddle. Duke was a very nice windmill.

*   *   *

The day of the game seemed endless. I woke up, first thing, and said, "I wish we were playing at one o'clock this afternoon." A nine P.M. start is torture.

The kids ate breakfast—same breakfast buffet, same omelets, same scrambled eggs, same room, same tables, same, same, same—and were their usual selves. I didn't see anything that indicated that this was *the day*. I, too, did not have the feeling that THIS WAS THE DAY.

I was a little surprised by the lack of that feeling. I was really looking for it during the Ohio State game, waiting for some giant gargoyle to sit on my shoulder and play my nerves as if they were strings on the first harp in the Boston Symphony Orchestra. There was nothing. The feeling, really, was that this was just another game. I'd coached a lot of big games in big arenas. Maybe I hadn't coached this one before, but I'd coached a lot that seemed just like it. We wanted to win. Period.

I was up to 810 games as a Division I coach now. That's a lot of basketball. I never, not once in all those near misses in the NCAA tournaments, never, had the feeling that if I didn't win it this time around, I'd never have the chance again. I just don't think that way. I always figure there'll be another chance. If we didn't win the national championship one year, then we'd win the next year.

I probably wouldn't want to coach a game where you said I was going to die that Friday. Or "the world shuts down on Friday and you can never coach another game." I don't know how I'd react to that. I've always been a believer in that old saying, "Failure is success turned inside out." If it didn't happen today, well, it would happen down the road.

It wasn't until we went to the late-morning shoot-around that I even thought there was something special about playing Duke. Everyone else was excited about it. Ask any of the kids—they all wanted Duke. None of them wanted Michigan State to win in the semis. Our fans wanted Duke because of our NCAA history, a chance for revenge. The general public wanted Duke, so that the two teams that had shared the No. 1 ranking during the entire season, finally would get to meet each other. I was the only one who truly didn't care. I wanted us to be in the final, I wanted us to win the final, but the opponent really didn't matter.

Only on the way to the shoot-around did it hit me . . .

"Yeah. UConn versus Duke.

"Yeah. This is the way it should be.

"Yeah. This is the *only* way it should be."

I guess I was late to the dramatics of the event.

●   ●   ●

I was at an interview, so I missed the moment when Kevin Freeman turned into the heavyweight champion of the world. The shoot-around was done, easy stuff, just getting loose, and the kids had showered and dressed. I was in the press conference area, unloading my last clichés before the big game. Sort of like getting rid of ballast. The kids and assistants were waiting for me in the locker room.

Kevin took off his shirt. No one knew why. Kevin is a big kid, built the way some Hollywood spokesman would have you believe you'd be built if you sent in those three convenient payments of $19.99 each and received that magic machine and accompanying video.

"I see no way they can win the fight tonight," Kevin said.

What?

He started to jab, shadow box.

"I'm pretty. I'm the greatest."

Jab. Jab.

"They're going dowwwwwwwn."

The other kids started laughing. Khalid and Ricky are our usual clowns. This was different. Kevin? The other kids took up the words.

"I see no way they can win tonight," one kid said.

Jab. Jab.

"I'm pretty. I'm the greatest," another said.

Uppercut.

"They're going dowwwwwwwn."

Karl Hobbs told me, when I reached the room, that he wished the game were being played right now. We'd win by 15 points.

Duke would go dowwwwwwwn.

·   ·   ·

The schedule became a countdown, starting at five o'clock. The entrées for the pregame meal were chicken and swordfish; we had the same two entrées for every game we played this year. Why swordfish? I like swordfish. Simple as that. I usually don't eat with the team, and didn't now, but swordfish always was available. The assistant coaches eat the swordfish. The trainer, Joe Sharpe, eats the swordfish. Lew Perkins, our athletic director, eats the swordfish. I don't think anyone under the age of 30 eats the swordfish.

Two pots of pasta were on each table, one with meat sauce, one with marinara.

A pitcher of iced tea.

A dessert buffet.

We were on the bus at 6:30. I was there with my bad shirt. Pat was next to me. We were at Tropicana Field by 7:15. Same route. Same. Same. Same.

I did an interview early, as soon as we got to the arena, with Bonnie Bernstein of CBS. I said the usual, that it should be a great game, two best teams, blah, blah. I got held up when I was finished and was half listening while Bonnie did an interview with Khalid.

"We're going to shock the world," Khalid said, looking straight at the camera.

I'd never heard him say that before, but, OK, shock the world. It sounded all right to me.

Dave Leitao said someone had told him the one thing that any coach should do on this night was take five minutes, early, before everything started, and walk to center court and simply look around, take a deep breath, and record the picture. He did it, and Karl did it, and Tom did it, and I should have done it. I look at pictures now—Tim Tolokan, our associate athletic director for communications, has a big 360-degree shot of Tropicana Field that night—and I don't recognize anything. They could be pictures of the marketplace in Tangiers.

I was mostly busy with my normal pregame worrying. It's my ritual. *What if Richard has a terrible night? What if we just can't stop Brand? What if they run all over us, get us down fast, embarrass us in front of the nation? What if Khalid gets nervous? What if Jake gets hurt? What if a lightning bolt comes through the roof of the dome and strikes all of us dead?* Think about the worst, I suppose, and anything else will be better.

The NCAA works on a 60-minute pregame clock. The teams shoot and practice for the first 30 minutes, then return to the locker rooms. With

27 minutes left before the game, Joe Sharpe handed me my usual five sticks of Big Red chewing gum and two Certs. I put a stick of Big Red in my mouth, everything else in my pocket, and started chewing at the hyper sideline speed that would continue until the final whistle sounded. I talked to the team for the next five or six minutes.

There was nothing new, nothing different that I could tell them. I emphasized our strategic keys: to double-team Brand, to keep the ball out of William Avery's hands, to play hard defense, and to play a tight, controlled offense—not slow, but tight. I told them again that this was our time, that we should take advantage of it.

With 20 minutes to go, the players gathered in the corridor and said a prayer. Khalid led them, as he had done since his first game as a freshman, when he changed the old formal prayer and moved to a more personal conversation with God. Sometimes other players spoke, sometimes not.

Every kid on the team then started singing a song called "Ruff Ryders' Anthem" on the long walk to the floor. It is a rap song, sung by a guy named DMX. I like all kinds of music, but I admit that I got off the bus when rap got on. I tell the kids every rap song is the exact same song, except it's sung by another guy or three guys or sometimes a woman. The kids think I'm music-irrelevant.

I tried to listen to this song once, but it seemed to be a string of curse words and grunts. I suppose there is a melody in there somewhere. Our manager, Josh Nochimson, says, "It's kind of like 'Eye of the Tiger' was for your generation."

The kids started the season singing the song only near the dressing room, but with each success they had become bolder and bolder. This time they sang it all the way down the long corridor, out the dugout, and straight to the center of the Tropicana Field floor.

With five minutes left before the game, I went to the floor, followed by Dave, Karl, and Tom. It is always the same order: myself, Dave, Karl, and Tom. We do not sing.

I suppose, somewhere in that long day, even at the last minute, when the three officials came out, Tim Higgins and Gerry Boudreaux and Scott Thornley, I should have reflected on everything. I should have remembered the bus rides home from Colgate, the driver and I the only ones awake, him driving and me writing up a letter of resignation I never would submit. I should have thought about the climb, the quest, whatever it was that seemed to interest everyone else. I should have thought about the people, the players, the milestones. I should have thought about this great season, the convergence of so many good things, the unique cast that had brought us to this unique moment in a dramatic, unique way.

I never did.

I simply never would allow myself the luxury.

I didn't want to lose the concentration, the focus on the job at hand.

I never had the time.

But I do now.

Chapter 2

UCONN

Dear Jim,

I remember back just a few short years, to the summer of 1985, sitting in a dorm lounge talking with you about UConn basketball. You were about to start your first camp and you were interested to hear from a few local coaches about the state of basketball at the University.

There was no Huskymania and there certainly was no one who would have thought a national championship was possible. Maybe not even you. Over the years you put together the coaches and players who built the foundation and pushed your program all the way to the top. Taken as a single accomplishment, this year was truly magical; however, taken over your tenure at UConn, it is a masterpiece of labor, perseverance, and uncompromising drive.

Best regards,
Neal Curland
Norwich, CT

I was 44 years old when I lived with the cockroaches. That was my beginning at the University of Connecticut. I had a wife and two teenage sons and a pleasant house and a former life back in Dedham, Massachusetts, but I lived with the cockroaches at the Lakeside Apartments on North Eagleville Road in Storrs, Connecticut.

I hear the Lakeside Apartments are better now, but when I was there they were impersonal and grim. The other residents of the furnished apartments were mostly visiting professors, there for a week or a month or a semester to teach a little bit of Elizabethan poetry or macroeconomics. Some conference people would stop for a few days here and there, all the pharmacists from the Northeast, perhaps, gathered to discuss the complexities of the latex glove. The cockroaches seemed to be the primary tenants.

"Look at that one," I told Pat when she came to visit one weekend.

She shuddered.

"I bet you could put a saddle on him and ride him to Hartford," I said.

Actually, a cockroach would have been a more stylish mode of transportation than what I had. I drove a nondescript light blue sedan, issued from the state of Connecticut motor pool. There were forms to fill out, receipts to be kept, windows to be rolled down to keep the driver awake because there was no radio. A decal with the state seal was on each of the two doors so curious strangers would not mistake me for visiting royalty rather than a government functionary.

I shared the car with Dave Leitao, one of my new assistants, who lived next door with his own set of cockroaches. I often ate in the car, fast-food lunches and fast-food dinners, as I went around the state to talk to Rotary Clubs, Junior Chambers of Commerce, veterans' groups, and seventh-graders, anyone who would listen. I threw the fast-food papers and coffee cups into the well in front of the passenger seat. Leitao, on his own trips, contributed to the pile. We never cleaned.

"What kind of car is this?" I asked Leitao once.

"I think it's a Dodge," he said.

"What model?"

"I think it's a Dodge Shitbox."

I was 44 years old and I drove a Dodge Shitbox and lived in the Lakeside Apartments and I was the new UConn basketball coach. Welcome to the big time. The year was 1986.

*   *   *

I was the mystery guest. Sign in, please. I had arrived to reenergize, revitalize, resurrect, and restore an athletic empire that probably never had existed, except in people's minds. I was here to drag a great sleeping beast from the mud at the bottom of Mirror Lake or someplace and set it loose on the unsuspecting world. I was here . . .

I was here to win some basketball games.

I had been introduced to the public at a press conference at the old faculty-alumni center on May 15. I talked the way I talk now, kind of fast, the words warped by a pahk-yah-cah Boston accent, hard to understand if you're not paying attention. I acted the way I act now, kind of excited about what I do, but not as manic as I sometimes look on the sidelines. I guess I had the same kind of big ideas that I have now, except they were about a million light-years away from being fulfilled.

Doable was the word I used at my press conference.

Sounded good.

"Dare to dream" was the message I delivered to the good Rotarians and the Boy Scouts of the Quinnipiac Council as I toured the state.

Sounded even better.

Let's see: I had given up a job that I loved at a place that I loved, Northeastern University. I had moved from a city that I loved, the place where I had grown up, a cosmopolitan city with the Red Sox and the Symphony, with the jogging track along the Charles River, with the Public Garden and the Common, with the hustle and bustle of commerce. I not only had left a house that I loved, but had left my wife with it, to close up all business before she came to join me with our sons. I had left friends. I had left extended family.

I had landed in a place where the biggest tourist attraction seemed to be the creamery at the school of agriculture. ("Have you tried the ice cream?" everyone always said. "Best you'll ever eat.") There was no hotel in Storrs, no place to buy a suit of clothes, no real sit-down restaurant, no McDonald's! The university was an outpost in the eastern corner of the state. A quiet outpost that I would learn to love.

My oldest son, Jimmy, was a freshman at Northeastern and liked the idea of switching schools, heading to a college that had an actual campus instead of buildings stuffed in between trolley tracks and office towers and urban decay. He was my one ally. My younger son, Jeff, in eighth grade, acted as if his heart, soul, and two or three molars had been extracted from his body. The only things he saw were cows and grass and a life he envisioned as something out of *The Beverly Hillbillies*. He wore his red Northeastern socks to the press conference in defiance and watched everything with a death-row disposition.

My poor wife didn't know what to think. Had her man lost his senses? She privately predicted that we would be here two years.

"Jim," she said at the press conference, looking at all the cameras and lights and people, "we don't know anybody in this entire room."

Dare to dream?

I guess I was taking up my own dare first.

*   *   *

My small office was on the second floor of the old Field House. The temperature in the spring and summer was about a billion degrees. The synthetic track on the floor of the building was made of some space-age substance that emitted a curious, foul odor. The odor never left, not for any minute of any day. I grew immune as the day progressed—"What's that smell?" a visitor would ask. "What smell?" I would reply—but every morning was a period of adjustment. It was like working in a tannery.

My three assistants, Leitao, Howie Dickenman, and Bill Cardarelli, were stuffed in an even smaller office on the same floor. They worked the telephones, calling the young basketball talents of the land, describing the potential paradise that awaited in Storrs. The phones they had to use were so old they had rotary dials. Dickenman said he lost 5.2 seconds on every call, matched against a Touch-Tone phone. He had timed out the difference.

As for me, I had meetings.

I had meetings with administrators, admissions people, basketball players, would-be basketball players, professors, students, and painters, whom I wanted to bring in to paint the walls of the locker rooms.

I had meetings about meetings.

For every academic who told me that the university wanted nothing less than kids who have 1,200 on their SATs, rank in the top quarter of their high-school class, are pre-med or pre-law, Rhodes scholar material, I had others who told me I should open up the waiver wire, take anyone and everyone, just as long as they're breathing. I had advice. I had a lot of advice. There even was a 66-page tome, the report of the President's Task Force on Athletics, filled with advice. I looked through that, searching for the key changes that would help this school become what it wanted to become.

The two big recommendations, as far as I could figure, were (1) buses for road trips should always be equipped with lavatories and (2) when the buses returned from road trips at night, they should bring the student/athletes to their individual dorms rather than drop them as a group at the Field House. OK. Come to Connecticut! We have lavatories on our buses!

The thing I liked best about the report, I guess, simply was that it existed, that somebody not only cared, but cared deeply. I decided that I was the one who was going to have to develop the program step by step, and convince all of these advisers that my way was the way to travel. It was my show.

"Jim . . . ," John Toner, the athletic director, said one day when he called my office.

"Yes?" I said into my black rotary-dial phone.

"You were clocked by a state trooper traveling 89 miles an hour the other day, driving on the Gold Star Bridge across the Thames River on I-95," John said. "The trooper let you go because you were in a state car with the state seal on the side. He called me instead."

I was on my way.

*　　*　　*

Three days after I took the job, I had attended a meeting of Big East coaches at Dorado Beach in Puerto Rico. It was a coincidence of timing, the meeting coming so soon, but that little gathering showed me how much work there was to do. The Big East, our conference, was the glamour conference of the country at the time.

I was sitting in function rooms with John Thompson of Georgetown, who'd won a national championship two years earlier, Rollie Massimino of Villanova, who'd won a national championship one year earlier, Lou Carnesecca of St. John's, who'd been to a Final Four, Rick Pitino of Providence and Jim Boeheim of Syracuse, whose teams would be in the Final Four at the end of the coming season, and P. J. Carlesimo of Seton Hall, who had recruited the foundation of a team that would be in the Final Four in three more years . . . these were the people we had to play.

Why were you speeding, sir?

Well, see, I was at this meeting at Dorado Beach . . .

*　　*　　*

I did know a bit about UConn basketball. I also knew a bit about winning. I'd been head coach at Northeastern, remember, for 14 years. I'd coached an All-American. I'd brought teams to five of the last six NCAA tournaments. It wasn't like I was some wide-eyed visitor from the Midwest, looking for the first time at the Tilt-a-Whirl at the state fair.

I'd been around New England basketball all of my life. I'd been to games at the Field House in Storrs. I'd *played* in the Field House in Storrs.

I knew that Connecticut was a basketball state—interest everywhere. I knew about the high schools: Hillhouse and Wilbur Cross, Hartford Weaver and Hartford Public, Bridgeport Central and Kolbe, and all the rest. I knew about the state legends, from Johnny Egan at Weaver to John Bagley in Bridgeport, Harold Pressley at St. Bernard's in Uncasville, and Super John Williamson at Cross—all those great players who had wound up playing at other schools around the country. I knew about the Horde, the great media marching and chowder society, the legion of sportswriters who chronicled every UConn double dribble in every newspaper in the state. I knew about the television exposure. I knew about the UConn regional tradition that went back through Corny Thompson and Tony Hanson and Joey Whelton and Toby Kimball, back to Hugh Greer and Vin Yokobaskas and Walt Dropo.

I knew about the great expectations.

I also knew about the losing.

· · ·

Almost one year earlier, my Northeastern team had played in the Connecticut Mutual Classic at the Civic Center in Hartford. I had seen UConn basketball up close, firsthand.

We had a good team at Northeastern, understand. We had been to the NCAAs three straight years and were heading there again. We had Reggie Lewis, All-American, in our lineup. UConn was coming off three straight losing seasons and heading to a 12–16 finish. The scene was still like . . . how do I explain it? We somehow still were the poor relations visiting the manse.

There was a crowd of 11,688, with the band, the noise, the whole thing. I come out and the three officials come out and they go directly to talk to Dom Perno, the UConn coach. OK, fine. They'll talk to him, then they'll talk to me. I'm waiting and waiting and they never come. I'm 14 years a head coach, it's December 28, and maybe they could come over and wish me a Merry Christmas or a Happy New Year or something. No, nothing. It's not an accident. It's UConn.

The game begins and they score. We bring the ball back up the court and our kid gets whacked, no call, loses the ball, and they score again. I go into my high-grade ballistic routine. Technical foul. They make the foul shots, keep the ball. I'm still ballistic. I go after my kids, not a hard role for me. We just kill UConn after that. We're up 30 at one point. We eventually win, 90–73, to win the tournament championship. Reggie scores a bunch of points.

I go to the press conference. I'm feeling pretty good about all this.

First question: "What's wrong with UConn?"

Second question: "How could UConn be better?"

Third question: "UConn . . ."

No one asks about us. Nobody asks about Reggie, about how great he was, about the fact that we played only seven kids and five of them were in double figures. Nobody wants to know. UConn, UConn, UConn. That's the whole press conference. It's all woe is me, Chicken Little, the sky is falling. There was only one team on the floor, it turned out, UConn.

I, of course, am no longer a happy coach.

Except, of course . . . wouldn't it be nice to have that kind of attention, that kind of passion around you every day?

*   *   *

I suppose that game that night probably brought me to the UConn job as much as anything. I know it stuck in the mind of John Toner, the athletic director, when he started to look for a new man. He talked about sitting at midcourt, next to the scorer's table, liking the things he saw Northeastern do, not liking the things he saw Connecticut do. I suppose that buzz, the feeling from that night, stuck in my mind, too, when I weighed making a jump from the familiar to the unfamiliar.

There had been other offers in the past. Nibbles. Flirtations. None of them seemed right. I was closest with Northwestern, which meant Chicago, the Big Ten. I talked about it with Bobby Knight from Indiana. He said that Northwestern was a graveyard, that no one could win at Northwestern. He preached the doctrine that all directional schools, schools with a *North, South, East,* or *West* in the name, were to be avoided. His advice was to look for a state school. The University of Something. State schools were solid. State schools had resources. State schools had instant, in-state fans.

Wasn't UConn a state school? The University of . . . Connecticut?

I'd never really wanted to move away from Massachusetts, to tell the truth. (What about that job at Stanford? Stanford? That's in California. Why would I ever want to move to California?) At the same time, though, I had begun to feel a little too settled. We had lost to Oklahoma in the first round of the NCAA tournament at the end of a good season, and I found that the loss didn't grind at me, kill me the way other losses in the NCAA had lingered in other years. One day, two days, I accepted it.

The downside at Northeastern was that the program probably never would be much more than it was. There was a limit to the heights that could be reached. When Pitino was coaching at Boston University we had a running joke that the games between our teams were for the 12th-place championship on the Boston sports scene. After the Red Sox, Celtics, Bruins, and Patriots, after Boston College (all sports), after Harvard football, after college hockey (all schools), after—I don't know, boxer Marvin Hagler and maybe the Mass Handicap at Suffolk Downs—came BU and NU basketball. No matter how well we did, 12th was the ceiling. There never was going to be a big arena, big crowds. Plucky Northeastern always would be plucky Northeastern.

When John Toner offered me the UConn job, a seven-year contract, he figured I would jump at it, that this was my big chance. I wasn't quite that sure. I wasn't certain that I *needed* a big chance. There's an idea I have, and I think it's true for a lot of people—you can be just as happy being a doctor in a small town somewhere in Maine as you are when you hang your shingle outside Massachusetts General Hospital. The big time isn't necessary. I already had a job with tenure. What college coach has tenure anymore? I had a promise that someday, when I was finished coaching, I'd become Northeastern's athletic director. I asked John Toner for two days to think about it all.

There was a New England Gridiron Dinner the night before I had to give my decision. I received an award, New England College Basketball Coach of the Year, a clock. The dinner was terrific. The funny thing, though, was I looked around and saw all these Northeastern people, all these New England people, people I really liked, friends, good people, and that strangely convinced me. I was treading water here, doing what I always had done. I was too settled.

The next day poor Jeff was wearing those red socks and we were heading to Storrs.

        ⚬   ⚬   ⚬

I met my new players, one by one.

One player—I won't use his name—had a long-running problem with substance abuse. He was gone. Another player, no name, came into my office wearing a baseball cap turned backward, Walkman headphones attached to his ears. He did not leave with his baseball cap turned backward, Walkman attached to his ears. He never talked to me that way again. Another kid, I can't remember his name, sort of a funny kid from England, nice but very lazy, came equipped with suggestions.

"Here's what I think we should be doing at UConn," he said.

"We?" I said.

"Yes, here are some things I think we should change. . . ."

The change was him. Gone.

I will say that the cupboard was not bare. There were a couple of good recruits, Steve Pikiell and Tate George, joining the program. There were some solid big men—a good guard in sophomore Phil Gamble and a potential star, 6'10" sophomore Cliff Robinson. He'd averaged 5.6 points per game as a freshman, but I thought he could do much more. He was a good kid with a good future. He simply had to know I meant business.

"Do you want to be in the NBA?" I asked Cliff when we had our meeting.

"Yes, I do," he said.

"I want you to be in the NBA, too," I said. "I want you to know that I am going to work with you, help you, do everything I possibly can to get you to the NBA. I am going to give you the tools, set up the structure, that will allow you to get there if you work hard enough. Do you understand?"

He said he did.

"I also want to tell you this," I said, lowering my voice. "Don't f——with me. If you f—— with me, I'll run your ass out of here so damn quick you won't know what the f—— hit you. Do you understand that?"

I have read somewhere that the use of profanity is supposed to be the sign of a small vocabulary. Maybe so, but whoever said that never has been a basketball coach. There are points in conversation where the use of a certain foul word or two simply puts the proper emphasis on what is being said. If I tell you, "I'd like you to get a rebound and I'd like you to box out," you might react. If I tell you, "You'd better get that f—— rebound and you'd better f——box out or I'll sit you on this f—— bench and no one will ever see your sad f—— face again," well, that might get your attention even quicker.

Cliff Robinson just finished his tenth season in the NBA.

.   .   .

Howie Dickenman, my top assistant, had been a member of the previous basketball administration. A number of people had advised me not to keep him, that he was attached to the losing and, right or wrong, he always would be stuck with that image. I had an open mind. He appears to be a gruff guy, plainspoken, but he is tremendously caring, a Connecticut guy whose father was a legendary coach at Norwich Free Academy. I liked the fact that he had stayed around for the month between the time

Dom Perno resigned and I was hired. He could have left immediately, looking for another job. He didn't, because of his loyalty to the program and the kids.

"So, what's been the problem here with basketball?" I asked him. One question.

"Well, there hasn't been the proper support at the school," he said. "There's a rift between the academic side and the athletic side, a feeling that athletics aren't important. There's . . ."

Here's the thing: He never croaked Dom Perno. It would have been the easiest thing in the world to say, "The last guy didn't do this" or "The last guy didn't do that," but Howie never said that once. He never laid the blame on someone who wasn't there. Here's the thing: That's why I hired him. If he'd defend his last boss, he'd defend his present boss. I liked that.

Dave Leitao was a no-brainer. I'd known him since he was 18 years old. He played for me at Northeastern, this kid from New Bedford who could jump out of Cabot Gym. I'd beaten on him as hard as I'd beaten on anyone, challenged his manhood about 62 times a day, and he'd always responded. He stayed and became an assistant after he graduated, a loyal piece of all our success, a preacher of the gospel of Jim Calhoun. I will say that I kept him hanging for a few days. I wanted to make sure he really wanted to do this, wanted all the work that was going to follow.

"You're sure?" I said.

"Sure," he said.

Cockroaches. Dodge Shitbox.

The third assistant, Bill Cardarelli, was a young coach at St. Thomas Aquinas High School in New Britain. I wanted someone who had a close tab on all the high-school players in the state. He was a nice, nice kid, a real good basketball man. He's still nice, the athletic director at St. Joseph's College in Hartford. I like him a lot. He just was too nice for my operation. He stayed only a year. I don't think he ever had seen anyone work the way I worked, talk to kids the way I talked to kids. He was a kind of touchy-feely kind of guy. I am not a touchy-feely guy.

I want my kids to know they're part of a family. I want them to know that I'm the one in charge of the family. Okay, the father. I want them to know that I love them, but I don't necessarily love what they do. This is an old-time family. I'm in charge of the clicker.

Don't be late for supper.

         •   •   •

Here was the battle plan:

1. Get the great in-state kids. Build a barbed-wire fence around Connecticut, get to know about the potential standouts at a grassroots level, those tall kids coming out of eighth grade, the ones with the particular buzz around them. Make sure those kids are aware of the state university and the possibilities that await.

2. Get athletes. This was the formula I had used for success at Northeastern. When I first took that job, I had what I called a good "MBTA Team," named after the Boston transit system. Everyone came from the local area, good high-school basketball players, mostly white, solid, set-it-up, run-an-offense players. After four or five so-so years in Division I, I found that speed and coordination, strength and height were more important than basketball fundamentals, which can be taught. I switched to athletes. This meant looking out of state, recruiting mostly athletes first. We became much quicker—pressing on defense, running on offense. We became much better.

3. Go national. There was no way to get the top Philadelphia kid against Villanova, no way to get the top New York kid against Syracuse and St. John's, no way to beat Georgetown for the top kid in Washington. UConn was often wasting its time along the Eastern seaboard, getting kids, but getting the fifth-best, sixth-best kids in a city, kids who had been rejected by their hometown schools. Why not try for the best kid in Utah, the best kid in Louisiana, the best kid in the state of Washington? Sell the Big East and all its glory in places where no one else was selling it.

4. Make UConn a place where kids wanted to go. Get the promised on-campus arena off the blueprints and onto the landscape. Establish a sup-

port system for academics; this would be very important. Earl Kelley, the UConn star a year earlier, had been charged by the university in a bizarre (and stupid) case that involved a starter's pistol and then had flunked off the team. Get some guidance here. Back up promises to parents that their kids would receive an education. Make this a special place.

5. Get good kids, plain and simple, the type of kids who mirror our desire to excel.

Get people involved.

Get a car deal.

Oh, yes. Get a few wins. Get the ball rolling.

* * *

The search for talent was constant, daily. If good kids were available, we were talking with them. No one probably ever sold the concept of what wasn't harder than we did. Negatives can become positives. Yes, they can— if you have a little imagination.

Georgetown, for instance, could sell a future with, say, Alonzo Mourning or Dikembe Mutombo.

"What we have for you is a chance to play against Alonzo Mourning and Dikembe Mutombo," Howie would tell kids. "You come to UConn and you can make your mark against those big names. Wouldn't you want to do that? Go against the best?"

St. John's could sell the glories of playing where Chris Mullin played.

"You can go to St. John's and be the next Chris Mullin," Dave would say. "Or you can come to UConn and be the first *you*. Why be measured by someone else's standards? Come to a place where *you* will set the bar, forever, that other people will have to reach."

Syracuse could sell athletic tradition, trading on the glories of football players Jim Brown, Ernie Davis, Floyd Little, talking about autumn Saturdays, a campus abuzz with excitement.

"You could go to a football school," Howie would say, especially to kids from the South who were considering football powers as their school of choice. "But UConn is a basketball school. Come to UConn and *you* will be the big man on campus. There's nobody bigger here than a basketball player. Now, maybe you'd rather go to a place where the quarterback was the star, where all the girls loved the quarterback, but for myself . . ."

Recruiting visits were a dance with the possible more than a walk with the actual. A visit to the Civic Center in Hartford; OK, this is where the bulk of the games will be played. OK? A mere wink at the Field House: "It's nice in there, really. Come on, we'll be late for our appointment at the library." A good dish of that good ice cream would be served. ("I remember one kid who we signed mentioned the ice cream in a newspaper story," Dave says. "He said he never forgot the maple walnut, I believe it was.") Even a trip to the agricultural barns was a positive. Some city kids never had seen a cow in their lives. "Check it out. Here's a cow. That fat thing over there? A pig. You ever eat bacon?"

I remember that other Big East schools would try to describe UConn as an isolated, barren land. Other recruiters would say the school was so far away "you have to take a helicopter to get there." We, in retaliation, sold Hartford as a bedroom suburb to Storrs. You want to smell the bus fumes, see a concert? Hartford, 15 minutes. Howie would pick up a recruit at Bradley Airport, seat him in a blue state car, put pedal to the metal, and travel the actual 30 miles at 70, 80 miles an hour. See? Fifteen minutes. New York is just down the road that way if you want to see the Knicks. Boston? You go the other way. Closer. Catch the Celtics. Larry Bird.

The plans for the new arena were a constant. The kid could even place his finger on the drawn and numbered seats where his family would sit for home games once the place was built.

A senior we inherited, Gerry Besselink, a good kid, saw the production one day. He asked to look at the plans.

"I saw these same plans when *I* was recruited," he said. "I guess they're not going to have it ready for me, huh?"

Shh.

The night before my first UConn season opened, I stayed up late to watch my old team play Louisville, the defending national champion. It was one of those midnight games on ESPN, the first round of the Great Alaska Shootout. Northeastern won, 88–84, a terrific upset, the biggest win in the school's history. I watched Reggie and Andre Lefleur and big Kevin McDuffie, all those kids I knew so well, hug each other and dance and roll around the faraway floor.

The next day we beat the University of Massachusetts, 58–54, with a more subdued celebration. Three days after that, in New Haven, in that mausoleum known as Payne Whitney Gymnasium, we lost to Yale, 77–75, in overtime. There was no celebration at all. Unless you counted Yale, which had beaten us once in the past 15 years. Yale was very happy.

I would like to say that the rest of the season was a grand climb, ruffles and flourishes, trumpets hitting the high notes at the triumphant finish, but alas, that was not the case. The rest of the season was a trip through the Donner Pass. The wheels kept falling off the Conestoga wagons.

Let's see. We lost an awful game early in the year at Boston University when we arrived two hours late because our bus was in an accident on the Massachusetts Turnpike. That was an experience. We came over a hill near Exit 10 and a car was stopped in the middle of the road. The bus driver had no options. He T-boned the car, sending it spinning. As we hit—I can hear this today—a woman screamed as loud as a woman can scream. We all thought she was in the car. We all thought she surely was dead. It turned out she had left the car and was screaming from the roadside as she watched the car being destroyed. BU was coached by Mike Jarvis—remember the name—and the BU administrators refused to postpone the game. We continued to Boston, where we lost, 80–71. I was the one screaming at the end.

We lost to Villanova, 66–51, in the Civic Center, seventh game of the season. We were trailing by 14 at the half and were booed off the floor. End of honeymoon. (What? One night in the Poconos?)

We lost to the University of Hartford, 49–48, in the first round of the Connecticut Mutual Classic. Our *Christmas* tournament. The *University of Hartford.*

All this happened in the first month of the season. And then things got worse. Much worse.

· · ·

The big blow came from a direction I never had expected. Cliff Robinson and Phil Gamble, our two best players, were declared academically ineligible in the middle of the season. Just like that.

Here I was . . . one of my main selling points was academics. "Send your son to us, Mrs. Brown. We'll make sure he gets an education. You can count on that." Now here was this academic disaster—there was no other word to describe it. How could this be?

There was supposed to be academic counseling for these kids. To think that you can take a kid from an inner-city environment somewhere, ask him to play big-time basketball with all the work that entails, hand him five classes, a full schedule, and then say "Go get 'em" is incredibly naive. UConn is an academic school. I like that idea very much. There is no back door, no general-studies curriculum, no place to hide people. You have to have a major, work toward a degree. You also need some help if you're playing basketball in front of 16,000 people every third night and practicing your brains out every day. You need study halls, guidance. Summer school is not a bad idea, so you can carry a lighter load of classes during the season.

"The biggest problem isn't even all the time you spend at games and practice," says Ted Taigen, our present academic adviser, a man as important to our program as any of our coaches. "It's the condition you're in after the games and practice. You work out hard for two, two and a half hours, and what do you want to do next? Most people would like to take a good nap. You're physically and mentally exhausted. That's the big problem."

Robinson and Gamble hadn't been getting good academic advice. I looked at their schedules. They both had taken a pre-med biology course. What were they doing taking a pre-med biology course? They weren't going to be doctors. The adviser at the time told me, "Well, it filled a requirement, and it was the only course available that fit their schedules." Unbelievable.

They hadn't failed for the semester, squeaking past, but they hadn't maintained a high enough cumulative grade point average, which was a tougher standard. I asked for a hearing, an appeal. I remember stating the case, saying these kids had had bad advice, that they were in the wrong courses, and that they still were eligible on the semester requirement. But the faculty judges weren't convinced and upheld their ineligibility.

That was it. I vowed that no kid on my team ever would flunk off the team again. (Only one has—a kid who simply refused to go to classes.) I convinced Robinson and Gamble to stay, even though other schools were buzzing around them, looking for them to transfer. I realized, more than ever, far more than at the Lakeside Apartments or driving the Shitbox, how hard this job was going to be.

This was the one and only time the word *doable* stuck in my throat.

* * *

As often happens when teams hit adversity, we had a terrific win in the first game after Cliff and Phil left the team. We beat Boston College, 66–60, at the Boston Garden in a nationally televised "Big Monday" matchup on ESPN. The two freshmen, Tate George and Steve Pikiell, played 38 and 40 minutes. A walk-on, Greg Economou, who really was a baseball player, played 20 minutes and scored nine points in the game of his life.

It was all a pretty illusion.

We had injuries.

We had more injuries.

A walk-on soccer goalie wound up joining the walk-on baseball player in the lineup.

We lost nine of our next 11 games for a 9–19 finish.

We finished last in the Big East for the regular season.

We finished last in the Big East tournament, eliminated in the dreaded

8–9 game by BC, 61–59, on Thursday at Madison Square Garden before the other teams had even arrived for the quarterfinals on Friday.

●　　●　　●

Dare to dream? This was a dream after a fat bowl of firehouse chili and maybe a banana split. The 12–16 year of the previous administration had been turned into 9–19. Nice progress.

Who was this Calhoun guy?

How could he keep talking the way he talked?

These were pretty good questions.

Chapter 3

Dear Coach,

Congratulations! Unbelievable!

All the guys from Dedham used your run to the national championship as an excuse to keep in touch. Joe Keaney and Jeff Dillon were interviewed by the *Boston Herald.* I was interviewed and appeared on Channel 4, WBZ, 6 P.M. news. I even predicted a three-point win, but that part was edited out. As a result of your win, obscure high-school players, 27 years later, get to be minor celebrities and have a small role in your ride. . . .

Your coaching philosophy still remains . . . hard work and pressure defense. All of us who played for you and know you from Dedham lived and died with you during your tourney run. . . . Sure beats driving to West Point, N.Y., in 1970 in a Plymouth Duster with four high-school lads . . .

Bill Littleton
Worcester, MA

The worst story my father ever told me when I was a child was about himself.

He was a teller of stories, my father, five times around the world with the U.S. Merchant Marine. He told me about London and Paris, about the Orient, about being bitten by a camel in Egypt. To this day, if I ever am about to go to one of these places and people ask, "Have you ever been there before?" my answer is yes. I was there many times as a child, transported by my father's words.

The worst story took place closer to home, in East Boston, Massachusetts.

My father's family lived on Bennington Street or Porter Street or Maverick, one of those crowded East Boston streets, while he was growing up. He was one of seven kids. His father was a banker, treasurer of the Sumner Savings Bank, a civic leader, secretary of the East Boston Catholic Literary Guild. He had immigrated here from Ireland. One day when my father was 15 years old, coming home from school through the rows of three-decker tenements, a neighbor yelled to him.

"Hey, Jimmy Calhoun," the neighbor yelled. "Your father just died."

The message was true—my father's father had died of a heart attack at age 45—but how could someone deliver it in such a cruel way? To be free and happy, a kid, and to have someone tell you something like this, shout it at you, to have your life changed in an instant . . .

I always thought this was the worst story I ever heard.

        •   •   •

I loved my father. He was the dominant figure in my life. He was 6'3", slender, maybe 175 pounds. He was athletic, good-looking, and could still throw a heavy fastball, even into his fifties, when we played catch. There was a presence to him; he was one of those men everybody noticed when he walked into a room. People liked him. He was a supervisor at the gas company, president of the Fraternal Order of Eagles in Weymouth. A joiner. A leader. He was everything I hoped to be.

I loved just being around him. When he smiled, it was like the sunshine had broken loose on a cloudy day. When he raised his voice, you snapped to attention, because he didn't raise his voice too often. I'm sure he never read Dr. Spock in his life, but he sure knew a lot about how to be a father. He had both a sternness and a gentleness to him that amazed me. One look from him was enough to know what he was thinking. If he gave you praise, which he didn't do often, you knew it meant something. You had to work for his praise.

We lived in East Braintree, a workingman's suburb south of Boston. There were six kids in this family: my two older sisters, Rose and Margaret, my younger sisters, Kathy and Joan, and my little brother, Billy, who was 11 years younger than I was. It was one of those old-time Irish Catholic families. As the oldest boy, I was called "the King." Billy was "the Prince." Those were our nicknames in the house. My mother, Kathleen, was 10 years younger than my father. She was sweet and funny. I always think of her, somehow, when I see the actress Goldie Hawn. She had Goldie Hawn's disposition. I think she gave me a sense of humor and a positive outlook on things—you know, the ability to look at a piece of shit and see it as fertilizer rather than as . . . well, a piece of shit. I loved my mother, of course, everybody loves his mother, and I idolized my father.

From about the age of six, my happiest moments came on Saturdays, our day, when he was all mine. He took me with him wherever he went. A lot of the times he went to sports. He loved baseball, loved football. He didn't know much or care much about basketball, which he never really had played. Basketball wasn't a big sport in Boston when he was a kid.

On those Saturdays, often as not, we'd go to Fenway Park in the summer. He'd talk with everyone, talk with the pretzel guys and the program sellers, everyone we met. I go there now and I think about all that. In the fall we'd go to Weymouth High School football. Weymouth, the town next to Braintree, had a big-time high-school football team. Weymouth High, the kings of Massachusetts football! That was their reputation. I remember listening to the radio as Weymouth beat Edison High of Miami, Florida, for the national championship when I was 9 or 10 years old. Every Saturday in the fall, my father would go to the games with four or five other men and me. We'd meet the other men at Arthur's Deli for breakfast, talk about sports, events of the world, anything, then go on the road to Everett, Medford, Brockton, Lawrence Central, wherever the game might be. Brockton-Weymouth was the big game on Thanksgiving. There'd be 25,000 fans at Legion Field in Weymouth. I could still describe Legion Field, every detail, today. It seemed like the Rose Bowl to me. After the games we'd go to the Eagles, to a tavern somewhere, and the men and my father would have a couple of drinks, shooters, and I'd have a Coke or something. They'd let me play the shuffleboard machine. It was what you did: go to the game, a couple of drinks, home. A man's life. This was what a man did. I was included.

·   ·   ·

There was a field behind our house that everybody called "the Polliwog." The town later did some work and renamed the field Faxon Park, but to the people in the neighborhood it was always the Polliwog. I played every sport possible in the Polliwog—baseball, football, hockey. There was a rink in the Polliwog.

My father would come to my games, Little League and all that, but he wasn't one of those sports fathers, getting involved in the politics, talking with the coaches, the whole thing. My father would stand by himself behind the center-field fence and watch me play. That was his style. Little League was very political at that time . . . you know, if your father was the coach, you probably pitched or played short and batted third or fourth. My father's idea was that you went and played and did your best and made your own way rather than having someone make it for you. It was one of those early lessons: Just do it yourself. Take care of your own business. He gave me a lot of those lessons, simply by the way he was. He probably didn't even know he was giving them sometimes. Or maybe he did.

An example: There was a shortcut that I always took through the Polliwog to come home. One day I was walking along the shortcut and four or five older kids stopped me. They said they owned the path and I couldn't use it anymore. Kid stuff. They slapped me around a little. I wasn't stupid. I didn't use the shortcut anymore. I took the long way around to get home after that. Somehow, after a while, my father noticed that I was taking the long way around. He knew there was something fishy.

"Why are you going that way?" he asked. "Why aren't you taking the direct way, the way you always used to take?"

"I don't know," I lied. "I guess I like the long way better."

"No, you don't," my father said. "There's something strange here. Tell me about it."

Eventually I told him the story. Right then, that moment, he took me back to the Polliwog, to the shortcut. The kids saw us coming, this large man and me, and started running. My father told them to stop, that he wasn't going to hurt them. I had no idea what he was going to do.

"You want to fight my son?" he said. "That's fine. Here he is. Pick out one of you and he'll fight. Then he'll fight the next one and the next. I don't have any problem with that. One-on-one. Now, if you want to fight him five-on-one, well, that's another matter and I'd have to be involved. But one-on-one, come on. Here he is."

I guess one of the kids stepped forward and I guess we had a fight, but I remember that everyone lost interest pretty quick. Funny thing, I wound up being really good friends with some of those kids, played on teams with them. We're still friends today.

It was a lesson, though, wasn't it? You don't have to take the long way. No one can make you, if you confront the situation instead of run from it. I've tried never to take the long way again, in case you haven't noticed. I go straight down the middle.

•　　•　　•

Sports were never too hard for me. I had a little bit of size, and that helped. I made the age-group teams and did pretty well. I added basketball to my plate in seventh grade when I was spotted by Fred Herget, a local elementary-school teacher who also was the coach at Braintree High.

Fred Herget was a coach who was ahead of his time. He didn't have a team; he had a program, a system, whatever you want to call it. He was thinking about basketball for the entire year, not only when the next season arrived. He was the head of the parks and recreation department in the summer and his players were counselors at the playgrounds and he drove around, making sure each kid was taking the required number of foul shots, working on whatever weaknesses the kid might have. He also always was looking for young kids, talent that could be developed by the time it reached the high school. I was one of the kids he found. He encouraged me to get involved in basketball. He paid attention to me.

I, in turn, found that I liked basketball. I liked it a lot. The solitary qualities of the game, the practicing by yourself, appealed to me. You know the thing everybody does, taking shots, making up the play-by-play in your head? I liked that a lot. Johnny Most, the phleghm-filled radio voice of the Celtics, shouted in my head, described my many wonderful moves. *Calhoun scores again! Can anyone stop him?* I tried to make the moves fit the description. I practiced basketball by myself, even during football and baseball seasons, when I was playing for other teams. I became a pretty good shooter.

In eighth grade my team won what we called the state junior high school championship of Massachusetts. It really wasn't the state championship, because the teams were only from the eastern part of the state, but who cared? The game was in the Boston Garden and we won, South Junior High of Braintree against Shirley Junior High of Everett. I wasn't the leading scorer, but I had 18 points and did all right. My dad was in the stands. He didn't say much, just congratulations, but my mother told me he was almost in tears when he got home and described what he'd seen. It was the way he was.

———

•　　•　　•

At that time, though, baseball still was my first love, probably because there was a field behind our house, probably because it was the sport everybody played in the neighborhood, probably because it was my father's first love, too. In the summer of 1957 I was on a Babe Ruth all-star team. I was 15½ years old. There was a game one day at a local field and I was in center field, waiting for fly balls. A neighbor—I won't use his name—came from behind me and yelled over the fence.

"Jim," he said, "your father's dead. You better go home."

The cruelty, the lack of common sense, again amazes me.

What was this guy thinking?

The worst story I'd ever heard was now also my story.

•　　•　　•

I suppose everyone has a moment somewhere that shapes his life forever. This was mine. I talk about it now, more than 40 years later, and I can still feel the way I did then. I remember my legs were weak as I walked off the field. I went home in a state of disbelief, not knowing what to expect, not knowing what was next.

Indeed, my father had died of a heart attack, same as his father. He had left a widow and six children, almost the same as his father. He was 53 years old, eight years older than his father, still dead way too soon. It was almost too much to comprehend. My mother was in the living room at the house. Some neighbors had gathered. My brother and sisters were there. Fred Herget was there. I walked over to my mother and—I don't remember saying this, but all my sisters swear I did, so it must be true—and I said,

"Don't worry. I'm going to take care of you."

I mean, where did that come from? I was 15½ years old. I couldn't take care of myself, much less anyone else. *Don't worry. I'm going to take care of you.* I didn't even know what that meant, what it entailed. I must have invented it because I was the oldest son, something I probably figured I should say. I had no idea.

And yet . . .

How would I describe myself today?

I would say that I have a great feeling of responsibility for the people around me. I would say I have a great sense of family, family in the broadest sense, including my best friends and my teams and the people around my teams. I always have thought that was how I would be judged, by how I took care of the people around me. Even now my wife will tell me that I'm anxious before games because I know my family is in the stands and I don't want to disappoint them, don't want them to have a bad experience at the game and then a long ride home. I argue with her, tell her that's not the case at all, that I'm anxious because we're playing against Alonzo Mourning or a team with six McDonald's All-Americans or something, but you know what? She's more than half right.

I have that feeling of responsibility.

I'm doing what I think my father would have done.

I started when I was 15½ years old.

*   *   *

The changes in our lives after my father's death were subtle but significant. I'd say we were comfortable when he was alive. He didn't make the most money in the world, but he did well enough to provide basics and extras, to keep things going quite well. There was not as much money after he died, and my mother, bless her, was not the greatest manager of it. Her spirit, her optimism, her presence were what kept us together. We weren't poor, not at all, but we certainly were far from rich.

I talk with a lot of kids from tough situations now, go into their homes, and I think I can understand. I think I can relate. I know what it is to have to work as a kid, to bring money home to help the family. I know what it is to lose a father. You can talk all you want about race and differences, about a white man going into the home of a black kid some-where, selling the advantages of a particular college, a basketball team, but economics and life experience are a strong common denominator. If you've known hard work and loss, you are speaking a common language with other people who have known hard work and loss.

The death of my father put me into a spin. I probably didn't think so at the time, going through high school, having some friends, having a girl-friend, playing three sports, but I look back and see that it had a large effect. I lost interest in a lot of things. School, for instance. I became a C student who just didn't care. I internalized a lot. I was a shy kid—yes, true, ask my wife, I'm still shy—and I kept to myself. I was never the talker in the crowd. I was a fighter—tell me to go f—— myself and you'd have a go f—— yourself back, maybe with a fist in the face—but I was never in the front of any discussions. I suppose playing sports was the place I felt most at ease. I knew the rules.

I worked and I played sports. Those were my major activites. I worked in a bunch of places. I worked in a junkyard separating scrap metal for the Fore River Shipyard. I made candy for Peachy Candy. I worked the fair circuit with a guy from the neighborhood, the Marshfield Fair, Brockton, Weymouth, worked in the paddock area. I worked on a truck, delivering product. On a Saturday morning I'd work 6 to 10 at a gas station, then somebody would pick me up and I'd play football for Braintree High in the afternoon. I kept a busy schedule.

Fred Herget, the basketball coach, became the one father figure in my life. He was a tough guy. I won't argue that. If you screwed up, he let you know it. He'd stand behind you at practice, and if you missed a shot and didn't follow it to the basket, he'd give you a not-so-gentle nudge. Just like that. Coaches couldn't do that now, but they sure could then. And he did. I'd miss a shot, not follow it, and feel the nudge coming. I didn't mind, though. I guess I was looking for discipline. I found it with Fred Herget.

He got me one of those jobs as a playground director in the summers. He came around and made sure I was taking my 200 jump shots or what-ever. He had me playing in summer leagues and on teams. He gave me organization, structure. His trademark was his red socks. He always wore red socks. Come tournament time, Braintree would be in the thick of it, led by Fred Herget and his red socks.

I became a pretty good player. I was picked as an All-Scholastic in football by the *Quincy Patriot Ledger,* the newspaper for the South Shore, and I played pretty good baseball, but basketball was my sport. I had grown to 6'5" by the end of my senior year, and I could shoot the ball, so I was an All-Scholastic in this sport, too. In today's times, with coaches and scouts everywhere, I would have been recruited by someone, offered a college scholarship. In those times, the early sixties, the interest in the game wasn't as great.

I talked with Dave Gavitt, then an assistant at Providence College. I talked a little bit with Jack Leaman, the assistant coach at the University of Massachusetts. I had scholarship offers. Nothing ever was finalized, put on paper. I also talked with my mother. She was hospitalized for a bit at that time, suffering from angina. My two younger sisters were still in high school. My brother was only eight. I realized that I was needed most of all at home. I didn't go off to college with everybody else, heading straight toward that American Dream.

Responsibility. I got a job.

*   *   *

There is a difference between a real job and one of those jobs you work while you're in school, trying to make a little money to have some fun. Do you know what I mean? There is a finality to a real job. You get up, do your 8 or 10 hours, come home, have supper, waste a little time, go to bed, get up, go to work again. I worked first at a company in Quincy, dispensing electronic equipment, then I moved for the big money. I worked for Settimelli Stonecutters in Quincy. The average workday started at 5 A.M., and I cut stone, did sandblasting, managed not to kill myself, and came home, covered with dust, looking like I'd just survived the bombing of Dresden.

My friends would return from school for vacations, go back, and I kept cutting stone. I made new friends, older friends. I gave half my paycheck to my mother, kept half, and played basketball after work with every team I could find. I was still young, 18, 19 years old, playing with older men, guys who had gone to college and come back. I played for the Trigger Burke Club, the Whouley Club from Hull, the Koch Club of North Quincy— different leagues, different tournaments every week, every weekend. I went out after the games with my teammates.

It was a seductive life, a trap. How many young guys fall into it without even knowing what happened? There is a murky plan to go to college, to do something, but today is today and tonight is tonight and tomorrow can be worried about tomorrow. Maybe a girl gets involved . . . there's a baby . . . end of story. You wake up one day and suddenly you're 35 and your temporary life is your permanent life. I didn't want to go there.

Enter Fred Herget again. Actually, he never had left.

He would call me every couple of weeks or so, push me, prod me. He'd say things like, "I hear you were up at the Squire Tavern the other night. You aren't letting these guys suck you in, are you?" He kept telling me that I had to go to school, to do something. Talk about a coach. Isn't this advice about a thousand times more important than "Follow your shot to the basket"? This is what it's all about: loyalty. He didn't forget you simply because you weren't on the team anymore. You were in the system forever. That's a coach. I like to think that I would have gone back to school on my own, but I don't know. With him in the background all the time, there wasn't a choice.

Today, if you ask me who my mentor is, I'd have to say I really don't have one. I didn't start out as someone's assistant who then became someone else's assistant and then became a head coach, sort of like Roy Williams at Kansas, who began as an assistant to Dean Smith at North Carolina. If I'm a product of anyone, it's Fred Herget. He showed me what a coach should do, what a coach should be. My whole coaching philosophy comes from Fred Herget and my background, my family, with maybe some ideas from John Wooden's book on pressure defense.

I worked for 18 months after I got out of high school, and in a lot of ways I wouldn't trade that time for anything. I learned a lot about responsibility, about family. I also learned that I didn't want to work as a stonecutter for the rest of my life.

I caught a break at a weekend basketball tournament in Holyoke, in the western part of Massachusetts. I scored 40 points in a game, and Bill Callahan, the coach at nearby American International College in Springfield, saw me. He took an interest. Someone told him that I was only 19 with four years of eligibility.

"You should come to AIC," Callahan told me. "You'd be good with us. We'll give you a scholarship."

"I'd like to do it," I said. "But I have to work. I have to help my family. I have responsibilities."

"How about this?" Callahan said. "We'll get you a job at Milton-Bradley in Springfield making toys. You can work during the day and start AIC in night school. We'll go from there."

I was off to college. Just a little late.

*   *   *

The school turned out to be perfect for me. AIC was very small. People knew who you were and everyone seemed to care about you. There was an incredible family atmosphere. I wasn't the only one who had come to the school on the rebound. A lot of people had. AIC was that kind of place. Moose Stronzak, who became a small-college All-American in basketball, had arrived after a year at Holy Cross after a run-in with the administration. Everyone seemed to have a reason why he wound up at AIC.

I only know that the school and the school life felt natural to me from the start. I climbed out of the aftereffects of my father's death and was much happier than I was in high school. I joined a fraternity, Zeta Chi. I made friends for a lifetime. What's the old joke—"College was the five happiest years of my life"? Well, if you add in the 18 months I was working, I guess I would say, "College was the six happiest years of my life"—I was at AIC for a while.

"Calhoun was the same way he is now," my friend and roommate at Zeta Chi, Bob Samuelson, says. "He was self-assured. Very confident. In the front of everything. Wanted to be the leader of the pack, king of the hill. I'd have arguments with him—I still have arguments with him, getting into it pretty good—that were something to see. He was confident, but not to the point of being arrogant. I'm sure down in those dark places he had those insecurities that we all have, but he didn't show them."

I was a sociology major and an English minor. I was a basketball player, averaging 14 points as a sophomore, 21 as a junior, 14 as a senior. (When I was a junior, we played on the road at UConn. The game was in the Field House. I scored 27 points. Check with Tim Tolokan. He has a copy of the box score. December 1, 1964.) We had good teams, college division, made the NCAA tournament for the first time in my senior year.

Samuelson, who was a backup guard on the team, says that I never played defense, that I shot every time I had the ball, that the only passes he received from me hit him in the head because he never expected me to pass. I don't know about all that. Maybe those basketballs that hit his head did something to his memory.

I worked all the way through school. Even though I had a full scholarship, I still needed money. Callahan helped, getting me jobs. One of them was to clean the uniforms. Great job. I'd score 25, 30 points, come back to the locker room, take off my uniform with everyone else, take a shower, then pick up my uniform and everyone else's and do the laundry while the rest of the team went out to celebrate. Kids bitch to me about their hardships at UConn . . . well, this is a story they hear.

When it was time to graduate, I wasn't ready—still short a semester, maybe a semester and a half. I suppose I would have liked to play some more basketball somewhere, but there really weren't any opportunities. I wasn't an NBA guy, not good enough for that. Europe was a possibility. I suppose today, same circumstances, I probably would have taken a shot at Europe, but at that time there was very little money for basketball in Europe, no real demand for American players. The old Eastern Basketball

League was around, but there was no money and no real future there. What was the point?

I was better off trying to finish off my degree. Callahan, the coach at AIC, suggested that I come back, finish up, maybe start on a master's and be an assistant coach. It sounded like a good idea to me. This was 1967, and that Vietnam War was cranking up, and a student deferment alone seemed pretty good. I liked the student part of the deal better than the coach part. I truly had no idea that I wanted to be a coach. I never really had thought about it, hadn't taken one phys ed course. I didn't know what I would be.

I had met Pat, my future wife, one of seven kids in her family, during college. She was a Weymouth Landing girl, the first girlfiend I'd ever had who actually was a friend as well as a girl. We talked about everything, anything, and laughed a lot. We'd drive to Cape Cod and back for fried clams, just to talk with each other. It was a little surprising that we hadn't known each other as kids, growing up, except for the fact that she'd gone to Catholic schools and I'd gone to public schools.

She mentioned one time how she'd received First Communion at Sacred Heart Church. I said I'd also received First Communion at Sacred Heart Church. We talked about the dates when we'd each received Communion and figured out that we'd received it together. Her mother still had a home movie. Sure enough, we looked at the movie and, at the front of the line, there was this lovely little girl in her white dress and veil. At the very end of the line there was this tall, skinny gawk, white suit, hands folded.

Fifteen years later we walked down that same Sacred Heart aisle and Pat took a job with AT&T in Springfield, and I took the AIC job and the chance to finish my education. And a funny thing happened. The first time I put that whistle around my neck for that first practice, I knew what I wanted to be.

Nothing ever had felt more right in my life.

•   •   •

How do you know that you're doing what you're supposed to be doing? How do you know you have found the place where you fit best? Say you're a banker. Is that what you're supposed to be? What if you had become a farmer? An electrician? A concert pianist? How do you open the door that's right for you? Is it luck? Happenstance? Trial and error?

I don't have the answer to any of those questions. I somehow found the right door, and after that I just put one foot in front of the other. From day one, whistle around the neck, I never looked back and I never looked forward. I looked at whatever was the problem for the given day. I liked what I was doing and I kept doing it.

"What's the best career path to follow to become a Division I coach?" is a question I get asked at clinics.

"I have no idea" is my reply.

I suppose there is a path now, each job leading to a better job, a way to network, to move ahead. I suppose there was a path then, too: go to the 5-Star Camp in the summer, meet Hubie Brown, some famous basketball guys, hear about jobs, all of that. I had no idea it existed. Didn't have a clue. A network to me was ABC, NBC, the Peacock. My father watched the game from behind the fence in center field, remember? I was not built to be political. Just do the work. Something will happen.

I think about it: how many guys have great plans, get fired, bounce from one place to another, zigzag their way across the country looking to move ahead? I never had a plan, a grand design of any kind, and I not only never have been fired, the blowtorch never has been close to my ass. If anything, I've been the one holding the blowtorch on myself.

It's all kind of amazing to me, really. I don't know if you could go the way I did now; I don't think it'd be possible. I suppose my advice is that there *is* no career path, that you do the best you can at what you're doing and someone will notice. Is that too simple? It's what I did.

I was 25 years old when I got my first high-school job as a head coach. I don't think that could happen now. You'd need more experience. I was 29 years old, coming from high school, when I got my first Division I college job. I'm sure you couldn't do that now.

If there's a path here, it's certainly been covered with some dense underbrush since I took it.

。　　　。　　　。

Coach Callahan told me about the job at Old Lyme High School, on the coast of Connecticut. I'd finished my degree and was working on a master's in psychology. I was antsy. I was coaching the freshmen and felt I wasn't learning much.

There was a struggle going on, too, for the athletic director's job, between Callahan and Gayton Salvucci, the football coach, whom I did like. I didn't want to get mixed up in that. It was a good time to leave. The birth of our son, Jimmy, had taken Vietnam out of the equation. I was available. Hello, Old Lyme.

(A word about Vietnam: I was against the war. I was a Democrat, a liberal—still am. An AIC professor, Dr. Ken Weintraub, got me interested in politics; he was a fascinating guy. Bobby Kennedy had been shot, induction notices were going everywhere, and kids I knew from Braintree were being killed, and Weintraub just started asking me questions: What did I think about this war? Did I know anything about it? Did I think we had any purpose being in a Southeast Asian country? He made me come up with answers. I didn't go for the anti-American stuff, burning the flag, because I truly love my country, but I also wasn't in favor of the war.

My one trip to the induction center to be classified for the draft was interesting. The sergeant in charge of everyone came up to me and said, "Calhoun, how tall are you?" "Six-five," I answered. "You'd make a good lookout," the sergeant said. He started laughing. Big joke. He was laughing, and I saw my head sticking out of the jungle, snipers zeroing in. "You'd make a real good lookout," the sergeant said again. I tell my son—he's 31 years old now—that he was my antiwar protest, the result of a quick disregard for the old Catholic rhythm method. I was classified as married, with child. I also was a schoolteacher, another deferred category.)

The first day at Old Lyme I went looking for basketball players. It was

June, the start of the summer. I pulled up at the outdoor court behind the firehouse. Two kids were playing against each other. I watched for a while, then went over. The game was nothing, slow motion.

"What are you guys doing?" I asked.

"I'm a co-captain of the high school team," one kid said with a smile. "We're practicing."

"Well, I'm Jim Calhoun and I'm the new coach," I said without a smile. "Have everyone on the team back here at this court at six o'clock tonight."

I think four kids showed up.

Old Lyme was a rich town, a soccer town—always good soccer. The basketball team was terrible. It had a 29-game losing streak. I charged in with the Fred Herget game plan, trying to organize, trying to recruit, trying to get things going. I remember the soccer coach, Jim Gardner, a good guy, saying, "What are you trying to do, steal everybody from my soccer team?" I had a lot of energy.

I wasn't too much older than the kids I was coaching, but I had no problem telling them what to do. I never had trouble with that. *Never take the long way around. Straight through the middle.* I established from the beginning that I was the boss. I got a summer league going, captain's practices, the package.

I remember our first game. I still was playing a lot of basketball—played every day, in fact, one-on-one against the kids. I came out to shake hands with the opposing coach. He was much shorter than I, and slender. I thought, *I'd post this guy up. Destroy him.* Well, it didn't exactly work that way. We weren't the ones playing the game. The small, slender guy's team threw a press on my team that came out of a textbook. I think the final score was something like 90–45. If you ask my assistants today what my biggest worry is, they'll tell you it's the full-court press. Our teams have more ways to break a press than any team in the country. We kill a press, because I'm still afraid.

The team eventually finished 8–12, the most improved team in the league. Pat and Jim junior and I lived in a mansion for most of the year, a summer home that we sublet from some Hollywood producer, a guy whose wife had a radio show, *Stella Dallas.* The setup was terrific. The rent was $100 a month. For a mansion. The only thing I hadn't figured on was the heat, which was $300 a month.

I covered that with a second job as a constable in the town. I was a wonderful constable. They gave me a hat and a gun, the whole thing. The gun made me nervous. (Why? I do have a temper, remember. Think of how nervous referees would be if they saw me with a gun on the sideline.) I took the bullets out and hid them at home. I suppose it was really stupid—I mean, if someone pulls a gun on you, you probably should have bullets in your own gun—but it made me feel better. I'd break up altercations, a couple of guys punching at each other, but when the motorcycle gangs would show up at the beach, I'd go around the corner and call the state police.

I could have stayed at Old Lyme, I liked it, except I learned that to continue at the school I had to become a certified Connecticut schoolteacher. Since I never had earned education credits, this meant I'd have to enroll in courses at Willimantic State College. I was thinking about doing that, but then Pat's brother, an assistant superintendent of schools in Westport, Massachusetts, told us that the basketball job was open at his high school, and the new coach did not have to be certified.

Okay, Westport.

*   *   *

Again, we lived in a beautiful place. Westport is in the southeastern corner of the state, on the water, sort of tucked between Rhode Island and Cape Cod. Again, I inherited a terrible basketball team. Again . . . no, this time, maybe the only time I've ever coached anywhere, I felt my limitations.

Westport was a small school in an area full of bigger, powerhouse schools. There wasn't a lot of basketball talent in the town, but again there was a lot of money. There were the rich kids and the Portuguese kids. The rich kids had no inclination to play the game. They went to the beach. The Portuguese kids were short. I seriously doubt anyone could have won at

Westport, going up against teams from New Bedford and Fall River, schools with double and triple the enrollment. I was charging ahead, putting in the program, but there were serious doubts it would take us anywhere. The team's nickname, the Villagers, didn't even sound very tough. Our record in my first season was 1–17. The one win was by two points.

When Fred Herget (that name again) called at the end of that season and told me that the job in Dedham, a middle-class suburb outside Boston, was open, I was typing out my application before he even finished. I was ready to go.

One interesting postscript to my time in Westport is that one of my players was a kid named Steve DaCosta. He was my big man, a 5'10" junior. He grew up—despite whatever counsel I might have given him—to be a sportswriter, sports editor of the *New Bedford Standard Times*. He recently wrote a column about that Westport year and included a letter that I had written to him at the end of the season on the back of a copy of the team's grim statistics. This is the letter:

Steve–

We made these statistics. Only *we* can change them!

    You must improve all aspects of your game. I expect you to be our leading rebounder and need at least 12 points a game next year. You must work hard by yourself (every day) and try to gain experience against good players every chance you get. Also, as cocaptain, you must get the rest of the boys to play as much as possible. We need your leadership. Pride in yourself and us is what you must develop.

                        Coach Calhoun

P.S.–Save this as a reminder of what we must do!

I showed this letter to Dave Leitao the other day. He said, "This was written in 1970, but you could have written it to one of our kids last Thursday. It's exactly the same stuff you're saying now, 30 years later." I felt the same way.

No change. I like that idea.

I also like the fact that Steve DaCosta followed my suggestion and kept the letter. It's okay, Steve, you can let it go now. You also can stop practicing that jump shot.

·   ·   ·

Dedham was my basketball laboratory. Dedham was where I could take my Fred Herget Kick-in-the-Butt, 365-Day Formula for Basketball Success and lay it on an unsuspecting adolescent public. Dedham was a replica of Braintree, filled with tough little sons of tough Irish fathers. Dedham was a place where all of this would work.

The school was good in every other sport except basketball. Football was good, baseball was good, hockey was wonderful. Hockey was everything. This was the time of the Big Bad Bruins, Stanley Cups, Bobby Orr, and Phil Esposito. Every kid in town had that bumper sticker—Jesus Saves . . . and Espo Scores on the Rebound—in his bedroom. Every kid wanted to skate in the Boston Garden in a black-and-gold jersey, not dribble in a pair of black high-tops.

I just had to change all that.

I roared through that town like a missionary selling a place in heaven and a cure for acne. I made basketball easier to play than not play. I was persistent. I became the director of the playground program in the summer, and I got players jobs and gave them programs to follow and offenses to learn. I set up teams, leagues, championships. I bought trophies, raised money for shirts. There were three great full-court basketball courts in the center of town, and I kicked off those street hockey kids—*You want to make something of it, kid? I'm in charge*—and brought in basketball kids. I was ruthless.

I had my kids playing on Monday nights, Tuesday nights, Wednesday nights, Thursday nights, and Sunday nights. I had our Dedham High team playing in an open league, a college league, a Sunday-night shootout, all comers welcome. It all was legal. The rule was that I couldn't coach any of those teams, but, yes, I could watch the games. Were there any restrictions on where I could watch from? No. I stood a foot away from the bench. I couldn't coach, but I guess I could cheer. Or not cheer.

"Calhoun," another teacher at the school told me once, "you're the only guy I know who gets excited about what he has for lunch."

I looked up from my meatloaf sandwich and smiled.

Dedham, in two years, became the summer home for Boston schoolboy basketball. Ronnie Perry came from Catholic Memorial, Mark Young from Brookline. The best kids in the area played in Dedham. Against my kids. We had a good player named Jeff Dillon and some other pretty good kids, tough, and they all became better. The first year we finished 12–10 and the town was thrilled. We had a basketball team. The second year we finished 21–1, losing to a good North Quincy team in the state semis at the Garden. It was a local miracle.

I settled in for the long haul. I bought my first house. I went to every clinic I could find. I went to basketball camps as a counselor, sitting up late into the night, listening to longtime coaches like Don Tremblay from Lawrence Central and Henry McCarthy Jr. from Winthrop, John Killilea of the Celtics, the great former Celtic Sam Jones, talk about basketball and players, kids. I stole any basketball idea that made sense and put it into my own operation. I had no ambitions, really, except to stay where I was, to build a little basketball empire.

I had no idea I'd be leaving.

. . .

The month was September. The year was 1972. I was getting ready for my third Dedham season. We had a lot of good kids coming back from the 21–1 team. An assistant football coach at the school, Jerry Varnum, was a

Northeastern University guy and still was involved with Northeastern sports. He told me the athletic department at Northeastern had come up with a big problem: it needed a basketball coach in a hurry. Would I be interested?

Huh?

September . . .

Nobody needs a coach in September, especially a college . . .

Huh?

The situation was a mess. The coach of record was Dick Dukeshire, a Northeastern guy, a good coach who'd built a solid College Division program. He'd taken a sabbatical the previous season—now, that's something you'd never see today, a coach on a sabbatical, unless it was a perpetual sabbatical after a 4–28 season—to coach the Greek national team. A guy named Jim Bowman, his assistant, had replaced him. The plan now was for Dukeshire to return, Bowman to become an assistant again, everything to resume as normal.

The problem was that Dukeshire had returned in August and was sick. He had contracted a disease in Greece and would not be able to coach. The obvious answer was to retain Bowman as head coach for one more season, but Bowman had been offered a job by the FBI. His dream was to be an FBI agent. He already had been offered the job twice and turned it down to help out at Northeastern. The FBI had a rule, three strikes and you're out, so this was his last chance, and Bowman was going to take the FBI job.

The people in the Northeastern athletic deparment were in a panic. Not only didn't they have a coach, but they'd already applied and been accepted to be reclassified as a Division I basketball school. They were making this enormous jump, like going from welterweight to heavyweight, and they had no leader. They had reason to panic.

The job already had been offered to a number of college coaches. I know Gerry Friel at New Hampshire had been offered the job, as had Joe O'Brien at Assumption, Rollie Massimino at Stony Brook, a number of other people. Everyone had turned down the offer. Varnum said I should apply. Hey, look what I'd done at Dedham.

I applied.

I really was skeptical about my chances, but as the interviews proceeded and Varnum kept me posted from the inside, things sounded better and better. I remember saying to Pat one night, with a tone of amazement, "You know, I think they're going to offer me this job." It sounded like I was saying, "You know, I think Ed McMahon is going to pull up on the front lawn with that big check from Publishers Clearing House." Except I was right.

The football coach at Northeastern was Joe Zabilski, a terrific guy. He knew local sports and he told Herb Gallagher, the athletic director, "Hey, I know Dedham. They've never had good basketball. This guy came in, and two years later he's the Massachusetts coach of the year and the team's in the Garden. He's been an assistant at AIC, so he's been around the college game. He's worth the shot." Gallagher bought it.

I got the job on September 26.

The season began on October 15.

*   *   *

The first day, Zabilski handed me a travel budget, an equipment budget, and a schedule. That was the package. Notice that there was no recruiting budget. I had five scholarships, total, when the NCAA limit at the time, I believe, was 18. The schedule had been beefed up, building toward a full Division I program. I was making $13,800. I had been making $14,600 at Dedham. I guess I never was a captive of sound economics.

"Just do me a favor," Varnum told me. "Zabilski's a football guy. Herb's a hockey guy. Tell them how great it's going to be, but don't tell 'em how you are—you know, pushing so hard. Don't tell 'em."

At 29, I might have been the youngest Division I head coach in the country. I don't know. I do know there was a certain awkwardness. I was an AIC guy taking the Northeastern job. There was a bunch of Northeastern guys around the program—Ricky Weitzman at Peabody High, Ken Nolette at Norwood, Lennie Sorom at Waltham—who really would have liked the job. They weren't happy that an outsider, no experience, got it. There was a young assistant coach, Mike Jarvis—remember the name—a Northeastern guy, already at the school, who would have liked the job.

All of this sort of forced me to go my own way. There wasn't any out-and-out animosity, but there also wasn't a lot of help. I had to figure things out for myself. In the long run, it probably was for the best.

An example: I wasn't much older than most of my players, but I wanted to establish who was in charge. This was the early seventies, remember. There was a lot of hair. Guys had long sideburns, ponytails, beards, mustaches. I announced that we were going to look like a basketball team. Long hair was out. We were going to be neat and well groomed. We were going to be proud representatives of our institution. Neat and well-groomed representatives.

The next day the four black players on the team were waiting at my office. They all had Afros or facial hair. Sam Jordan, a great kid who wound up being superintendent of a house of corrections somewhere in Massachusetts, was the spokesman. He was about 6'4", with a scraggly little goatee and mustache that must have taken him 18 months to grow. He explained that this was a cultural thing, a comment about society, whatever. The four kids all said the Afros were important.

What to do? These were good players.

"Okay," I said. "We'll do this on an individual basis. I'll decide, for each player, what well-groomed means."

It was a lesson. I had made a blanket statement, which was wrong. You can't operate with blankets when you're dealing with a team of individuals, different styles. You'd better have a quilt instead of a blanket, because every piece is different. Afros were just fine.

●   ○   ○

I won't go into a blow-by-blow account of 14 years at Northeastern. I suppose I do that too often with my teams at UConn. The players at Northeastern have become the characters in my own little basketball mythology. *You think you're tough? Well, I had this kid named Mark Halsel. . . . You think*

I'm tough on you? Well, ask Dr. Keith Motley, still at Northeastern, Dean of Student Services and Student Affairs. He'll tell you how tough I can be. . . . You think you can shoot? You should have seen this kid, Perry Moss. . . . Perry Moss could shoot. You think you're good? Let me tell you about Northeastern. . . .

I'm a full-blooded American champion of the underdog. I like the Red Sox, remember. I cheer for the guy who has the fewest points and is trying to unseat the defending champion on *Jeopardy.* I still feel good, no matter how many times I've seen it, when Rocky Balboa goes the distance against Apollo Creed. Northeastern was just a wonderful, wonderful underdog.

There was no better feeling than traveling into the land of the rich and famous and rattling cages. While the Boston media might have ignored us, sending over the cub reporters or no reporters at all, there was no way to ignore us when we were in your face. Throw a basketball into the air and you had to notice us. The final six or seven years, when we got it going, were a grand crusade. The record in my final three years was 75–19.

Okay, four highlights:

1. The best thing that ever happened to us was the formation of the Big East. It sounds silly to say, because the Big East sapped attention from every other school in the East, but it forced the other teams to jump into other newly formed leagues. And these leagues had bids to the NCAA. We went into the ECAC North. We never had been given a Division I NCAA bid before, never close, but now, if you won the conference tournament in your league, you were Going To The Dance.

We won the league in 1981, finishing 24–6. The best team in the league really was Holy Cross, but we won it. That meant after we both had survived earlier conference tournament games, the league championship game was held at our place, tiny Cabot Gym.

The place was packed, maybe 2,800 fans, people standing in places where people never had stood, people on top of the Coke machines, everywhere. The game started 10 minutes late because Holy Cross had been caught in city traffic. My best friend in coaching, George Blaney, was the coach.

It was a close game, back and forth, but at the end Holy Cross seemed to have it wrapped up. A kid named Ed Thurman from Lynn was at the foul line with three seconds left. Holy Cross was ahead by a point. There was no three-point foul shot then, so if Thurman makes one, the best we can do is tie. If Thurman makes two, there is no way we can even tie.

He made the first. The Holy Cross bench started to celebrate. Even George started to smile. What could we do? We had two kids at the far end of the court, but what chance did they have of ever seeing the ball? Thurman then missed the second shot. A kid named Chip Rucker gets the rebound, throws the ball to Perry Moss. Perry is maybe 43, maybe 46 feet from the basket. He turns and shoots a jump shot, all in one motion. And there is never a doubt that it is going to go in. It was tracking, like one of those long golf putts that seem unbelievable. Through the basket. The gym erupts. People are all over the court. I, of course, am out there, throwing people out of the way, because all we've won is a chance to go to overtime.

In overtime, we win, 81–79. Perry Moss's shot still stands with any dramatic shot I've ever seen . . . and I've seen a few. To this day, people say that the noise from Cabot Gym and the noise from Punter's Pub, a Northeastern bar down the street, where the game was on radio, no television, was so loud that everyone in the area thought there had been an explosion. What other reason for so much noise?

2. We go from there to the NCAAs in El Paso, Texas. Al McGuire, the former Marquette coach and broadcaster, writes a column about how the tournament has become a farce, teams like Northeastern invited. He says we don't belong, that we can't compete against a school like Fresno State, our first opponent. Is this good for the locker room wall or what? We stay in a Holiday Inn at a truck stop with the Fresno State Red Wave band, which keeps us up all night. We go to the arena and there are maybe 8,000, 9,000 Red Wave fans in the stands. We have maybe 150 from Northeastern. The game is late, not even televised back to Boston.

Final score: Northeastern 55, Fresno State, 53. Thanks, Al.

3. The next year, NCAAs again, we upset a good St. Joseph's team in Uniondale, Long Island, then played Villanova for a shot at the Sweet Sixteen. I still say it was one of the greatest college basketball games ever played. We lost, 76–72, in triple overtime. There was a crucial over-the-back

call on a foul shot at the end against Dave Leitao that I have yet to see, no matter how many times I've looked at the tape. If we'd won, we would have played Memphis State with Keith Lee, a team I know we would have beaten.

4. One more year, another NCAA. This time, Reggie's freshman year, we beat a good Long Island University team in the first round, 90–87. I still don't know how we did that. That was a great LIU team.

Our next opponent was Virginia Commonwealth in East Rutherford, New Jersey. This was a game we *lost* on a last-second shot. The kid's name was Ronaldo Lamb. We were ahead by a point and we actually tip the ball, goes off a kid's hand, out of bounds, but the officials miss it and give the ball to Virginia Commonwealth. Ronaldo Lamb makes a great shot, no other way to describe it, and we lost, 70–69. I saw the kid sometime later on some religious show on television. He said that God delivered the moment to him, wanted him to make that shot.

"What about me?" I asked the television. "I went to Mass that morning. I thought God wanted that ball to be blocked."

Oh, well.

          •   •   •

These were some terrific moments, terrific memories. If these things happened today, with the increase in media coverage, SportsCenter around the clock, there probably would have been a lot more attention. We would have been underdog darlings. I might have been one of those coaches you see, the young guy on the rise, phone calls from schools around the country.

The way it was, we danced and went home and did the dishes. I learned that it's a curious feeling, going to the NCAA tournament. You go and you're part of it and you're all excited. The minute you lose . . . the absolute minute . . . it's over. The circus goes away with the calliope and clowns. You can't believe how fast it happens. It's like a big curtain is pulled across the stage. You're on the other side, saying, "Hey, wait a minute. Wasn't I just part of this? Where'd everybody go?"

The only way to stay with the circus is not to lose, to follow it to the end. I guess that's a large part of why I was listening when John Toner called from UConn.

I wonder every once in a while what would have happened if I hadn't needed the teaching certificate at Old Lyme. Would I still be in the Shoreline League, dean of coaches?

What if Dukeshire never had gotten sick in Greece? Would I still be back in Dedham at the high school?

What if Dukeshire had returned after his year of sickness and wanted his job back? Where would I have been then?

What if John Toner hadn't called? Would I have taken the big shot somewhere else? Would I have stayed at Northeastern for my entire career?

What?

I don't know. John Toner did call, and I answered. There was a chance to follow the circus to the end.

Chapter 4

THE DREAM SEASON

Mr. & Mrs. Jim Calhoun,

We were very happy and excited to hear that you became champions. Actually, we tried to reach you on the phone with no success. The newspapers in Israel were all covered with you and UConn winning the game.

We, as many others, feel the big winner is you, Coach Calhoun. We could feel your inspiration, and your fingerprints made all the difference.

Yael and Shai Sheffer
Ramat-Efhal, Israel

The phone call came on an ordinary day. A day like this. The spring of 1989. It is a crazy business, recruiting basketball players. There are kids you chase, embrace, smother with affection, and then they walk away from you, go somewhere else on a whim. There are other kids who fall into your arms, straight from the sky, and you're not exactly sure how.

Nadav Henefeld fell from the sky.

"Jim, this is Marv Kessler," the voice on the phone said. "How are you doing? Blah-blah. Good team you have up there, doing great. Blah-blah. Hey, would you be interested in the Larry Bird of Israel?"

Marv Kessler is an old-time New York basketball guy. He likes to call himself part of the New York City Jewish Basketball Mafia. He once coached at Adelphi. He coached at an assortment of New York high schools. He is a regular at the 5-Star Basketball Camp of Howard Garfinkle in Honesdale, Pennsylvania. I know he told his war stories late into the summer nights for almost 30 years.

The Larry Bird of Israel? I'd be interested in the Larry Bird of Mars.

"His name is Nadav Henefeld," Kessler said. "He wants to come to America. St. John's is talking to him now, but you never know. He's good, this kid. Six foot seven. A forward. Handles the ball. Larry Bird."

The kid apparently was serving his mandatory three years in the Israeli army, mostly by playing basketball for the Israeli national team. He was due to be released in the next few months. As a member of the army, he was legally forbidden to take money, but already his rights had been sold in the Israel club league to Maccabi, the biggest team in Tel Aviv. He was fighting the sale, even had hired a lawyer to sue the league and Maccabi. He was still an amateur and wanted to go to a U.S. college. Kessler said that if I was interested, I should call Nadav's lawyer in Tel Aviv, Zeissman.

I was interested. Zeissman confirmed Kessler's story. We talked for a while. I said that the signing period for a letter of intent had passed, so there could be no promises, but we both should keep in touch. A month passed. No word. Nothing. Kessler called again. An ordinary day. Day like this. He said Nadav was in New York, visiting St. John's. Nadav had met with coach Lou Carnesecca, liked the school well enough, but said it didn't fit into his idea of what an American college should look like. Jamaica, Queens, was a big city. New York. He wanted to see UConn.

We sent Dave to pick him up for a 48-hour visit, the one legal campus visit under NCAA regulations. Dave and Nadav drove the two and a half hours back, making small talk, passing the time, and then they came down route 195 into the campus. Nadav saw the rolling hills, all green, the library, the row of three houses of worship (Hillel House included), the dormitories. He smiled.

"Zees," he said, "looks like a college campus."

And so it began.

●　　●　　●

The 1989–90 season was not expected to be great. The Horde was typing out obituaries before the first turnover had been turned. I myself thought the landscape had changed for the better after my first three years at UConn, but what did I know? I lived in my own house now in Mansfield with my family. Jim junior had graduated. Jeff had flipped opinions completely, and now loved where we lived, playing basketball at E. O. Smith High School. The rotary-dial phones had been replaced by modern beauties with push buttons. The state cars had been repaced by personal vehicles. The on-campus arena was off the drawing board, under construction, scheduled to open in January. Wasn't all that for the better?

The predictions, alas, seemed to be the same as always in the Big East: eighth or ninth. Even the league's coaches, in a poll, picked us to finish eighth.

I didn't buy it.

I wasn't sure where we would finish, but I didn't think we'd be eighth or ninth. We were losing Cliff and Phil, the inherited anchors for our first three years, but I liked some of the younger players we had gathered together. We were more athletic than we ever had been. Taller. Quicker. Stronger. For the first time, I thought we could play the way I wanted to play, pressing all over the court, running people to distraction. We hadn't even put on the 2-2-1 press in the first three seasons, but it was going to be part of our standard game plan now.

We also knew something about winning.

The second season, 1987–88, had been a breakthrough in that respect. The regular-season finish wasn't great, ninth and last in the Big East, but a 75–62 win over Providence in the 8–9 game in the league tournament assured us of a 15–14 finish, even with a loss in the next game to Pittsburgh. A winning record—aided, no doubt, by the fact that we could bring people into the arena—gave us a berth in the National Invitation Tournament.

And then we won the damn thing.

It was a happy, unexpected roll that had the entire state dancing at the end. The NIT is supposed to be a losers' event, filled with teams that didn't make the NCAAs, but to us it was a fine debutante cotillion. Here we are. UConn basketball. Tate George hit a jumper in the lane at West Virginia to tie the game with six seconds and send us to a 62–57 win in overtime to start the ride. Cliff had 17 points and Phil had 16 in the next game, a 65–59 win over Louisiana Tech at the Civic Center.

The quarterfinal game . . . the quarterfinal game was magic.

The opponent was Virginia Commonwealth, God's team, which had beaten my Northeastern operation by a point in the NCAAs. The site was the Field House. The Muppet Babies already had been booked for the Civic Center, and George Thorogood and the Delaware Destroyers were playing the Richmond Coliseum, Virginia Commonwealth's home arena. The Field House was the only available option.

Never had so many people filled that old arena. (Smell? What smell?) The official crowd figure was 4,801, but somewhere the fire marshals must have turned their backs. People were everywhere, maybe 6,000 packed into the place. The court was covered with a smoky haze, kind of like those old boxing pictures. I even wondered if there was a fire somewhere.

"What is that?" I asked a janitor.

"It's from the noise," he replied. "There's so much noise in here that it's shaking the dust off the rafters. This has never happened before."

Cutting through the literal fog of UConn tradition, we dusted off Virginia Commonwealth, 72–61, then proceeded to Madison Square Garden, where we dumped Boston College, 73–67, and then Ohio State, 72–67, to win the school's first postseason tournament championship of any kind. It might not have played like a big accomplishment if you were Kentucky or North Carolina or Duke or somebody, but for our state it was a large step forward. Here we are. The tollkeepers on the Connecticut Turnpike applauded our bus as we passed on the way back to Storrs.

"I told you we'd come back with something positive if we had time and support," I told the state legislature when we were honored in Hartford. "Here we are. Hopefully, this is just the start."

I should point out that we had gone back to the NIT at the end of the third year, losing in the quarterfinals, but that somehow was old news now. Woe is me. The Chicken Littles were back.

•   •   •

I went to see this Larry Bird of Israel in the summer. In Israel. At the end of his two-day visit in Storrs, he had told me that he wanted to come to UConn. We had a strength coach named Jay Hoffman, Jewish, who had met and married his wife, an Israeli, when he was in Israel as an extra in the Chuck Norris movie *Delta Force.* Jay and Nadav talked in Hebrew.

Shalom. Shalom to you. It's crazy, the things that help in recruiting. A Chuck Norris movie.

Pat and I made the trip. It was a sketchy time. Tel Aviv was on some kind of alert because a fanatic had overturned a bus in Jerusalem and 20 passengers had died. There was a lot of unrest. I'd been to Israel once, but Pat had never been. We noticed the soldiers and the guns. Presumably the guns had bullets inside.

Our destination was maybe an hour and 45 minutes outside the city, to where Nadav was playing with the national team in the Maccabean Games. The cab ride cost about $100.

The game was terrible. The opponent—I can't even remember the country—was no match for the Israelis. Nadav was very good, but against the competition it was hard to judge. I did like the way he passed the ball and the way he floated on defense, stepping into passing lanes. He did, at this level at least, look a little like Larry Bird.

We talked, and he promised to meet me the next day at the Sheraton in Tel Aviv. He asked if Pat and I would have any problem getting back to the city.

"No," I said. "No problem at all."

I pride myself on my resourcefulness, my adaptabilty—probably too much. We stood outside this gym. Nobody spoke English. We didn't know what a cab looked like. Cab? Are you a cab? It was another $100 ride . . . eventually.

I went to the office of Zeissman, the lawyer, the next day. *I* felt like an extra in the Chuck Norris movie. There was an air of intrigue about this entire operation. Zeissman told me that some people would be very unhappy if Nadav did not stay home. Some people? He said there could be trouble. Trouble? He said people from the Israeli league probably would try to make sure Nadav stayed home. Zeissman asked if I was willing to fight for Nadav. When I said I was, Zeissman seemed satisfied.

Nadav came to the hotel. We established a nice relationship. Yes, he still would like to come. I told him that we wanted him. I said that one of the requirements for college in the United States was that he take the SAT exam. He said this was not a problem because he already had taken it. He was going to Australia to play for Israel in the World Under-22 Championships in August, but would be discharged after that and would come directly to Storrs. We shook hands.

Pat and I hired a guide and took a tour of the city. The next day we went home. She says I don't take enough time off for vacations.

Two days in Israel. Isn't that enough?

．　　　。　　　。

The player who excited me most for the coming season was sophomore guard Chris Smith. He was—and probably still is—the most important recruit in the school's history. He was the first blue-chipper since I had been here, and he also was our first prime Connecticut high-school talent. We had done everything right with Chris Smith. We had identified him early at Kolbe-Cathedral High School in Bridgeport. We had sold him on the idea of staying home to play in front of his mom, his uncle, his friends.

The day before he came for his visit on campus, we redecorated the assistant coaches' office—this was how important Chris Smith was. Howie Dickenman remembers rushing around furniture stores two days before Smith's arrival.

"I didn't know if I was supposed to rent furniture, supposed to buy furniture, what," Howie says now. "I just knew we need furniture. I talked with this salesman in the store and I said, 'I don't care about the color of the couch, I care about whether you can deliver it on Thursday. Can you have it there?'"

It was there. So was Chris Smith.

He wasn't a McDonald's All-American, but he was in the top 50, legitimate. He clearly was the best player in the state. I probably had played him too much as a freshman, because he made some mistakes that hurt us, but I thought that the previous year's sins would be this year's virtues. He had learned while he played.

Already his presence helped. Scott Burrell, a 6'5" forward from Hamden, had followed. Coming out of high school, he had been drafted in the first round of the baseball draft by the Seattle Mariners and turned them down to play basketball for his state university. He was—and probably still is—the most athletic kid we ever signed.

(A trivia question: Who is the only player in history who was drafted in the first round in both the NBA and major-league baseball? Scottie also wound up as a first-round pick of the Charlotte Hornets. He played minor-league baseball in the Toronto Blue Jays organization during the summers while he went to UConn.)

We had some experience with Tate George and Steve Pikiell. We had some slow-moving size with a couple of seven-footers, Dan Cyrulik and Marc Suhr. Suhr was a 7'1" kid from Cologne, Germany, whom we finally had gotten eligible. Another international project. We had some fluid size with 6'9" Rod Sellers. There were a few more good athletes in the mix, Lyman DePriest, Murray Williams, and Toraino Walker, a freshman from Orlando, Florida. There was a good little junior guard from Hillcrest Heights, Maryland, named John Gwynn.

John Gwynn made me laugh. He stuttered, but he always had great things to say.

"C-C-Coach, you're not so t-t-tough," he said once when he was a freshman. "You try to act tough, but you're really a g-g-good guy."

Then he caught the halftime heat a few times. It's easy to look at other guys, teammates, under an *f*-bomb siege and to smile about it. It's a different proposition when the focus is on you. The event becomes a bit more personal.

"C-C-Coach," John said. "I want you to know that I t-t-take that back. You're t-t-tough, all right. T-t-too tough."

I thought the sleeper in the package could be another recruit we had signed, a 6'4" kid from Toronto, Canada, named Phil Dixon. I thought he was going to be very good and could step in and help immediately. There had been some trouble in Canada, something with a girl, but it had happened when he was 14 years old (he was subsequently vindicated). He assured us that was all in the past. He seemed like a nice kid and already was on campus, participating in our CAP program, a preadmit program for students at risk, giving them an early jump on freshman English and math.

If Phil Dixon were the player we thought he was . . .

If . . .

I was on the road recruiting when I got a phone call. Phil Dixon was in another jam with a girl on our campus. It didn't seem like much, but I didn't like it. Not with the first incident. I flew home, talked to Phil, and told him it was over. I suppose he eventually could have done okay, and I still think he's a nice kid, but the newspapers were going to get hold of this and his life would have been miserable at UConn. I called Rick Majerus at Utah for him. He would be better off somewhere else.

We, however, would not be better off.

I'll admit I had a small feeling of despair.

How good would this Israeli kid be?

·   ·   ·

He arrived on September 1. Kessler, a good basketball man, said Nadav would be terrific, that he wasn't a big name yet in Israel, but he won everywhere he went, a star on the rise. Zeissman, the lawyer, had been a good player, a guard on the national team in 1979, the only time the country ever had won the Europe Cup, beating the Russians. He also said that Nadav would be great. Okay. Nadav was here. He had his scholarship. He only had to be admitted to the university.

"Do you have your SATs?" I said, putting the application forms together.

"Sure," he said.

Panic. He handed me the results. He was a very smart kid, spoke a couple of languages, but taking a test in a language that wasn't his own had dropped his score to 680. I think you needed a 700 at the time to qualify for a scholarship and be eligible to play.

The good thing was that he had time to take the test again. If classes hadn't started, a student could take the test again and then be admitted. It was all legal. Nadav had to find a place where the test was going to be administered this late, take it, pass it, start school, and be on the roster. He could play basketball informally with our kids while he waited, but couldn't practice with the team. No problem. He had an air of confidence about everything that almost gave me the same confidence. He would take some SAT prep courses. He would take the test. He would play.

"Where are you going to go to take the test?" I asked after a few days.

"I am flying to Dallas," he said.

"Dallas? You have to go that far?"

"Dallas," Nadav repeated.

He was going to *Dulles*—Dulles International Airport in Washington. He took the test at North Carolina State in Raleigh.

While we waited for the results, two large manila envelopes arrived at the office with postmarks from Paris, France. The envelopes were stuffed with documents claiming that Nadav was a pro. There were pictures of him on the court against club teams, the implication being that he had been paid. He hadn't. He simply hadn't. The allegations were not true. Despite the postmarks, this was a message about challenging the basketball system in Israel. The Israelis didn't want Nadav to fight the system.

I could understand their position. It was just a hassle for us. In the next few months I learned more about Israeli law, about NCAA regulations, about international students—eventually we had a folder that was about three inches thick. Everything, dare I use the word, was kosher. The Israeli league, in fact, later changed the rules. A kid in the service now has a choice of which team he will join when he finishes his military obligation.

The test scores came back on November 1. Nadav had passed easily. He was able to work out with the team for the first time that afternoon. That same night he played eight minutes in our first exhibition game against Marathon Oil.

And so it really began.

* * *

There is a basic, feel-good plot line to most of sports fiction. Think about the sports books you have read. Think about the sports movies you have seen. In the beginning, the team is in complete disarray, the laughingstock of the league. Ground balls go through infielders' legs, pucks zip past the beleaguered goalie's head (he usually wears glasses), basketballs are dunked in poor souls' faces, putts are missed badly, fistfights end at the wrong end of one-punch knockouts. What a team! About a third of the way through the production, some change is made: a new character appears, a new pitch is learned, a girl settles down a goofy, hard-drinking quarterback. *Voilà!* There is a period of adjustment, and then the team becomes better and better. Wins begin to multiply. Pages fly off a calendar, or maybe the names of cities are shown in rapid sequence on signs at the city limits as the team bus passes. There is music on the bus. Everyone is singing. Players who once hated each other now place whoopee cushions under each other's butt. Fans go crazy. The laughingstock becomes the conqueror. What a team! The credits roll across the picture of the celebration after the championship game.

This is pretty much what happened to us.

Take a little bit of, oh, *The Amazing Ducks.* Add some *Major League,* some *Bang the Drum Slowly,* and some *Bull Durham.* Maybe some *Tin Cup.* Certainly some *Rocky,* whichever Roman numeral you want. A good dose of *The Natural.* Maybe even a touch of *Flubber.* This was how our season unfolded, as if we were the Big East version of those Indiana high-school kids in *Hoosiers.* Old Gene Hackman was proud.

Nadav, it turned out, was our Robert Redford.

* * *

The first, ugly third of the movie started with the first game of the season, a 92–81 loss in the first game of the Great Alaska Shootout to a Texas A&M team that wasn't very good and would finish with a losing record. The ugliness surfaced again with a 64–57 loss to Villanova in the Big East opener at the Civic Center. The true ugliness, though, the bottom, was a

93–62 destruction at the hands of St. John's in New York on January 2, 1990. Our record might have been 10–3, but it was an illusion, stuffed with cotton-candy wins against Yale and Howard and Hartford and Maine and Southern Connecticut. The true record was 0–2 in the Big East.

We came home from St. John's at two in the morning. . . .

We practiced. . . .

Check that. The gym was dirty because a women's game had been held in the Field House that night, and the cleanup crew doesn't work until morning. I had the players sweep the floor, and *then* we practiced. . . .

I met after the practice with my assistants. The meeting lasted until dawn. . . .

We went over every player, everything we were doing. We questioned our basic philosophy. Our big innovation, the 2-2-1 press, didn't seem to be working. St. John's had killed it.

A headline in the morning paper said, "The Press Must Stop." Very clever.

I finally decided we should change nothing. The press would stay. There would be no adjustments. None. We simply would get after it, be more aggressive, work harder. We would stop f—— around. Foul word for emphasis . . .

It all worked.

◦　　◦　　◦

Nadav was the different factor in the ultimate equation. The more he played, the more familiar he became with his teammates, with the way we worked, the more the Larry Bird analogy seemed to fit. He had a presence, a leadership. "The Israeli Iceman" was one nickname he was given. He had a great settling effect on the entire team. He wasn't a great shooter, which was his weakness, but he somehow made shots that mattered. He was a terrific passer. He was the best off-the-ball defender I think I ever have seen.

He had a knack for knowing where the ball was going to go. He broke Mookie Blaylock's freshman record for steals. How could he do something like that? He was 6'7". Mookie was one of those quick little guards at Oklahoma. Nadav was just a fascinating player to watch. He had the Larry Bird gift of making everyone around him better.

We rolled off a 10-game winning streak after the St. John's loss. One week to the day after St. John's, we were avenging our loss to Villanova with a 71–54 pounding. On the road. Thirteen days after St. John's we beat fifth-ranked Syracuse, 70–59, another pounding, at the Civic Center. Seventeen days after St. John's we played second-ranked and unbeaten Georgetown. Top-ranked Kansas had lost earlier in the day, and Georgetown was going to become No. 1. Not really. The 2-2-1 press smothered the visitors at the Civic Center. The score was 14–0 before they even figured out how to get the ball upcourt. The final score was 70–65, UConn.

Twenty-five days after the loss to St. John's we played St. John's again. This was the first game at Gampel Pavilion, the opening—at last—of our new 8,241-seat, $28 million arena. Never again would we have to steer recruits clear of the Field House, afraid they might see some of the buckets set out on the floor to catch the drips from the leaking roof. Never again would we have to apologize to anybody. This was an arena that could compete with the palaces at any school in the country. And it seemed that we had a team that could do likewise.

UConn 72, St. John's 58.

No matter what we ever do, there will never be the same snowball effect, the same first blush of love, that surrounded this team as it barreled past one longtime obstacle after another. I would look into the stands and see dozens of Israeli flags being waved. The Star of David was everywhere. I would see people hugging other people in disbelief. The oh-my enthusiasm was infectious. People who never had paid attention to basketball in the state, much less UConn basketball, were paying attention to this team. There never had been anything around here like this.

We were 13th in the AP poll after the St. John's win. This was the highest the school ever had been ranked.

We were eighth a week later.

The players became something like rock stars. If they went to stores in

Hartford, restaurants, anywhere, they were recognized and mobbed. The biggest rock star was Nadav. He was our Elvis. He had Hollywood good looks, and love letters arrived by the sack. Every Jewish mother in the state wanted her daughter to marry this fine young Jewish boy. Every no-look pass, every win, increased the attention.

We were still eighth in the AP poll at the end of the regular season. We were tied with Syracuse for the Big East championship, the first time in the history of the school. We had finished seventh in the league a year earlier, the first time a team ever had made such a large jump in the standings. . . .

We played Georgetown in the semifinals of the Big East tournament, appearing on CBS national television for the first time in school history. . . .

We beat Syracuse, 78–75, to win our first Big East tournament title. . . .

We finished third in the AP final poll at the start of the NCAA tournament. We were seeded first in the East, the highest seed in history for a UConn team. It was the school's first appearance in the NCAAs in 11 years. . . .

There seemed to be a different first every day.

        •   •   •

The finish was two famous shots, two buzzer-beaters, the ball going through the net as the final horn sounded. Isn't that what the finish should be in any well-made work of sports fiction? There was one buzzer-beater for us, Tate George's wondrous heave from the corner to beat Clemson, 71–70, and send us to the Elite Eight. The other was Duke forward Christian Laettner's often-discussed jumper to beat us, 79–78, in overtime and send us home. They both happened at the Meadowlands, East Rutherford, New Jersey, and at least once a year, when we go there to play Seton Hall, I see them all over again. . . .

There is one second left against Clemson. We have squandered a 19-point lead. We trail by a point. We have the ball, but we are at the wrong end of the court. The kids, half of them, most of them, have surrendered to the inevitable. I am trying to whip them back to the moment, to make the best use of whatever chance we have. Scott Burrell, with his baseball arm, will throw the inbounds pass to someone at the other end of the arena. The logical choice is Chris Smith, our best shooter, who already has scored 23 points.

"Don't throw it to Chris," Tate tells Scotty. "Throw it to me."

Burrell throws the ball. Tate catches it, turns, and fires.

We suddenly are celebrating on the floor.

The flip side comes two days later. There are 2.6 seconds left against Duke. This is a back-and-forth fistfight. The lead already has changed five times in overtime. We have a one-point lead this time. Duke has the ball. There is a pass from Bobby Hurley, intended for Phil Henderson, but Tate steps into the path and intercepts. We have won the game! We are going to the Final Four! Tate cannot control the ball. It bounces out of bounds.

Duke has one last chance. Laettner, whom all of our kids call the dirtiest player we ever played against, throws the ball in bounds. He steps in bounds. The ball is returned. He catches. He jumps. He fires.

Five hours later I am back at Gampel Pavilion. The place is packed, people holding signs and cheering and crying. There have been signs of appreciation all the way from I-84 to the campus. I have never seen anything like this. I can hardly talk, hardly get the words out.

"Five hours ago, Christian Laettner broke our hearts," I finally croak. "You people have put them back together."

The curtain was closed. The team that was picked to finish eighth in the Big East finished with a 31–6 record.

●　　●　　●

Pete Gaudette, a friend, a longtime assistant to Mike Krzyzewski at Duke, told me not so long ago that Mike asked an interesting question once: "What if Tate George had kept control of that ball and it didn't go out of bounds?" Duke was probably the team of the nineties in college basketball, winning two NCAA championships, going to the final game five times. If Tate had held on to the ball, would that have changed the entire decade? Would UConn perhaps have been Duke? Would Duke have been UConn?

I don't know the answer to that, but I also don't care.

I, myself, don't deal in what-ifs. They will drive you crazy.

I know there are coaches who tear themselves up about last-second shots, staying awake and imagining different outcomes if the ball had been just a little off to one side, maybe half an inch, enough to catch a piece of orange-painted iron. I never have done that. What if Tate hadn't made that miracle shot against Clemson? He made it. That's what matters. What if Laettner had missed against us? He didn't. That's what matters.

What I know about the 1989–90 season, in the end, is that it established the future of Connecticut basketball. It was a skyrocket that pulled us to the place we wanted to be. Everything good that has happened since has been built on the foundation of what those kids did.

Our success in that season brought us exposure that we never had. It made us attractive to Donyell Marshall and Donny Marshall and Kevin Ollie and Brian Fair, kids from around the country who arrived two years later, recruited in the afterglow. The success of Donyell and those kids made us attractive to Ray Allen and Travis Knight, who then made us attractive to Richard Hamilton and Kevin Freeman and Ricky Moore and Khalid El-Amin. A cycle of excellence had begun. It probably really had started, bottom level, with the NIT championship, but this was an enormous boost.

The University of Connecticut won the Big East regular-season title six times in the nineties, five in the last six years. We won the Big East tournament four times, the last two in a row. We made the Sweet Sixteen in the NCAA tournament seven times in the decade, the Elite Eight four times. We won 257 games, lost 74.

What if? What-ifs can be strung across the sky, there are so many.

            ·   ·   ·

A few examples of what-ifs: The two big recruits, the two kids we wanted most, when the 1989–1990 season began were Billy Curley, a kid from Boston, and Dickey Simpkins, a kid from Fort Washington, Maryland.

Dickey Simpkins loved UConn. He wanted to go to UConn, noplace else. When he came for his visit the previous spring, however, John Gwynn and Lyman DePriest were his guides. They went to a party, our players met some girls, and they left the kid alone. Dickey Simpkins was pissed. We never could get him back. He went to Providence and then he went to the NBA. What if John and Lyman hadn't fallen in love?

Billy Curley . . . we spent months working on Billy Curley. We were convinced we had him. He was down to Villanova, Boston College, and UConn. We had a source, a guy who said he knew what was happening. He called and said that first Villanova and then BC had been eliminated, and that we should expect a phone call. There were high fives—semi–high fives, because it hadn't officially happened yet—among the coaching staff. We waited. And then we waited some more. The call never came. The source had been wrong. Billy Curley decided on BC, which was close to home. Then he went to the NBA. What if he'd decided the other way?

Ray Allen told us about a good prospect in South Carolina. He invited him to a game when we played at North Carolina State. The kid came to the locker room after we won. Dave gave him a UConn press guide. The kid held it as if he had been handed the Gutenberg Bible. He said he loved UConn. He played as a high-school junior in South Carolina and became known, then played his senior season in Chicago. Then he went straight from high school to the Minnesota Timberwolves. What if Kevin Garnett had come to Storrs?

Marcus Camby. It simply didn't work out. He was a Connecticut kid, late to draw attention, academically ineligible as a sophomore. I saw him play for the first time in the summer of his junior year at the ABCD camp in Long Beach, California. He made a move I never had seen from a big man. He was running down the court and a kid threw him a bad pass at midcourt; the ball was going out of bounds. Marcus Camby saved it, kept his balance to stay in bounds, then went around his back and made a pass to another kid. Marcus kept running and the kid passed it back; Marcus took two steps and dunked. I turned to Karl Hobbs, my assistant, and said, "How involved are we with this kid?"

It just didn't work out. I thought we had a chance. His mother said she liked us, but I don't know. His major adviser, Jackie Bethea, from the AAU program, didn't want him to go to UConn; she thought we never had paid enough attention to Hartford. Nothing against her. Nothing against him. He went to the University of Massachusetts and was college player of the year. Suppose we had been able to change his mind, somebody's mind? Would Marcus Camby have helped? Would we have won a national championship earlier?

Forget the what-ifs. What happens is what happens. Your record is what you are, and I like our record. I like our record a lot. I always have said—always will say—that success should be judged on a long-term basis. That is why I always have valued our Big East regular-season championships much more than our Big East tournament championships. More was involved. Much more.

The public legacy of Laettner's shot eventually grew to become "UConn can't get to the Final Four." Each time we reached the Sweet Sixteen or the Elite Eight, another entry was made to a supposed list of failures. I remember driving around Connecticut the day after Donyell missed those two foul shots in 1994 against Florida, the game we lost, 69–60, in overtime in the Sweet Sixteen. All the radio stations in the state were playing the sound of gagging, choking. I wanted to drive right to the radio stations and make a few disc jockeys do the sound effect live.

The legacy from the 1990 season is not Laettner's jumper and our disappointment at the end. Never was. The legacy is winning, success, putting yourself in the position to do even greater things. The legacy of 1990 is all the years building to 1999. The string of excellence, of good basketball.

What if?

I was in the fourth year of a seven-year contract when the 1990 season began. I have seen seven-year contracts become four-year and five-year contracts in a hurry, buzzards gathering on the trees. We were picked to finish at the bottom of our league. I finished the season as the national college basketball coach of the year. I signed a new four-year rollover contract.

What if a New York guy hadn't called and told me about "the Larry Bird of Israel"? All I know is that he did.

• • •

This time I was not there when the call arrived. I was in Carmel Valley Ranch in California at a Nike Coaches trip in the summer. The red message light was flashing on my phone when I came back to my room. I immediately became worried. The message light could only mean bad news. Pat wouldn't call unless some problem had arisen, because I call her every day. The kids wouldn't call, because I also call them every day. I was nervous when I checked with the front desk for the message.

It was from Israel. Nadav.

I called the number. Nadav cried as he told me that he had signed a professional contract with Maccabi. There hadn't been any indication of this, no rumors. He had fallen in love with a UConn girl and had taken her back to Israel with him. We were going to be picked to finish first in the Big East. Only Tate was gone from the basic lineup; everyone else would be back. Nadav was supposed to be back.

He never did tell me the reason he was leaving. We talked for half an hour. There were stories, later, that speculated he had used UConn, never intended to go to school any longer than a year, that this was his protest against Maccabi and the Israeli professional basketball structure. I don't think so. Another Israeli, Gilad Katz, was coming to school the next year. He and Nadav already had put down a deposit on an apartment together. This was August. Why would he have put down a deposit on an apartment if he'd been planning to leave?

I think the Israelis were smart. They used pressure on the family and on Nadav to come home and play for the national team. Nadav's mother had died of cancer when he was very young and he very much lived for the approval of his father. The father was a quiet, stoic kind of guy. That was his nature. I remember when he came over here and went to some games. Nadav was very excited; he would point out things, talk about his life and his new celebrity in America. The father would nod. He did not say much. It wasn't a bad thing—Nadav wanted his father to be proud of him, and the father *was* proud, but he just didn't show it. He wasn't a hugger and slapper. It wasn't his nature.

"It's what I deed," Nadav said on the phone, talking about signing the contract. "So I deed it."

End of explanation.

I was sad for a long while after he left. It really bothered me. I thought he could have done some great things here. Everything was set up for him. I liked him a lot, liked being around him. It was fun to see America through his eyes, new and different. He was so important to our team, so important to our psyche. He was something special. There would be other kids who would follow him from Israel—Doron Sheffer was terrific for us—but the Stars of David, the Israeli flags, disappeared when Nadav left. I never saw another one in the crowd.

I'm not sad anymore. There's a sweetness to his story, a magic, the way this character came out of the East to change everyone's lives, then disappeared. Was he really here? Did it really happen? I kind of like the way it ended.

Dare to dream? The Horde put a label on that 1990 fairy tale, called it "the Dream Season." I kind of like that, too.

Chapter 5

THE TRIP

To Jim Calhoun,

We watched your game against the Blue Devils from the land of the Tasmanian Devils. We've been following the Huskies since Bob read X rays at the UConn Infirmary and Windham Hospital. We gave up touring time and requested a late checkout so we could watch the big game.

> Bob and Betsy Birchenough
> Cleverdale, NY
> (in Tasmania)

I owned the key to the city of St. Petersburg, Florida, site of the 1999 NCAA Final Four, before the season even began. All we had to do—we being the University of Connecticut basketball Huskies, coached by Jim Calhoun, "the best coach NEVER to reach the Final Four"—was get there and I could use it.

Nice thought.

The key originally had been given to Bowie Kuhn when he was the commissioner of baseball. Now, retired from the game, he lived in Fairfield County. He apparently no longer needed to unlock doors around the home of the Tampa Bay Devil Rays, Tropicana Field, or at assorted spring-training complexes in the area. He had given the key to the nuns of the Franciscan Life Order in Meriden as part of a charity donation. The nuns had given it to me.

I guess they figured I needed the key to the site of the Final Four as much as any long-suffering soul on the planet.

I had met the nuns in 1988, after our NIT championship, when I spoke at their sports banquet in Waterbury. I went there, another dinner, another night; didn't know what to expect. There were about 400 people in a hotel ballroom, and Floyd Patterson, the former heavyweight champion of the world, was the other speaker. I remember he read his entire speech, word for word, off little index cards—very well, actually.

The night turned out to be a hoot. I gave my speech, and 10 or 12 nuns came up to the stage and and sang the Husky Fight Song. They were cute, funny. I met Mother Shaun Vergauwen, the founder of the order, and she was wonderful. I don't know what the exact prerequisites are for sainthood, but I would nominate her in front of anyone else I've ever met. There is a sense of peace and order about her that you can just feel. She told me about the Franciscan Life Center, about the work the nuns do, the hospice, the help they give to all kinds of people. I went home on a cloud, carrying a jar of cookies the nuns had baked.

"You can't believe these people, how great they are," I told Pat. "I was proud to be a Catholic. I can't remember the last time that happened."

The night and the experience actually brought me back to church on a regular basis. I'd never left, but there were Sundays when I'd miss Mass, a lot of Sundays. Not now. I never missed. I still don't. I found that if you look, there are places where the liturgy can become truly meaningful. I became involved with the nuns, helped them with their dinner, did whatever I could. I became friends with Mother Shaun.

At the start of the 1997–98 season, I made a promise. I told Mother Shaun that if we got there, she and another nun would come, as my guests, to the Final Four in San Antonio.

Uh-oh. We didn't make the Final Four. Again.

I immediately reinstated the promise for this year, and that was how I came to be the owner of Bowie Kuhn's key to St. Petersburg. Mother Shaun saw a certain symbolism here. I, in turn, gave the key to Pat for safekeeping. She, in turn, decided to bring it with her to every game this season.

For luck.

       º   º   º

The previous season had ended one stop short of San Antonio in Greensboro, North Carolina, in the East Regional final: North Carolina 75, UConn 64. There was the usual editorial tendency to lump this close, no-cigar finish with the other close, no-cigar finishes—Woe is me. One more time—but the truth was that it was a lot better than I'd expected it would be.

We had a very young team, starting one junior, three sophomores, and a freshman. The idea that we could put together a 32–5 record, best in

UConn history, Big East championships in both the regular season and the tournament, would have been tough to sell to me at the start of the season.

The sad fact was that we were out of gas by the time we reached the game with North Carolina. The kids never felt it—they felt they were going to win every game, no problem—but I felt it. I could see it. We had used up all of our energy getting to where we were. We were riding on the fumes.

Richard Hamilton's foot was sore. Jake Voskuhl's foot was sore. Kevin Freeman's back ached. I had that feeling we were done; I just didn't know if the feeling meant anything. Have you ever heard a coach say before a big game, "I think we're going to be great, obliterate the other team, cut down the nets at the end?" That isn't the way human nature works. Everybody says something like, "Well, you know, for us to beat this team is going to be an incredibly difficult task. Half our team came down with smallpox, and the other half has poison ivy, and I myself feel a cold coming on." You prepare yourself for defeat that way, in case it happens. A self-defense mechanism.

I wondered if that was what I was doing—maybe we'll be OK, after all—but the way we played against Washington in the Sweet Sixteen game told the true story. We led by 10 or 12 points most of the way, but weren't sharp. We made a lot of mental mistakes. Washington put in the big guys down the stretch, whittled away at our lead, and then, with 28 seconds left, took the lead by a point. We called time-out.

I'm not a hold-the-ball guy at the end of games. I don't believe in that. I think you score any way you can, then play tough defense. I don't like to play for the last shot unless it's absolutely necessary. It was absolutely necessary here. I thought we were gassed, gone. We couldn't play tough defense. Not even for the last 28 seconds.

So we held the ball, held the ball, and with about 10 seconds left, took a shot. Jake took it, missed, and then there was a tip and another and another, four tips in all, I think, and then the ball landed in Richard's hands and he made the fallaway jumper as the horn sounded. Everyone ran onto the floor and it was great, but over on the side Kevin Freeman was lying down and couldn't get up. We had to pump two or three bags of saline into him. We were shot.

In the regional final, I should mention that North Carolina was pretty good. It was, after all, ranked No. 1 in the country, with Antawn Jamison and Vince Carter—pretty good players. The fact that the game was in Greensboro, the stands filled with Carolina blue, also didn't help. Except we were done. It didn't matter. We gave at the office all year and there was just nothing left to give. You know what I mean?

I stood in the locker room, the kids crying, and I wanted to thank them. I wanted them to be proud of all they'd accomplished, because they had accomplished a lot. At the same time, though, I didn't want them to feel satisfied. I really couldn't give them the praise they deserved.

"I want you to remember how you feel now" was my message. "I want you to take this feeling with you when you leave here. I don't want you to lose it, how bad you feel. I want you to keep it for the entire year. Live on it. Feed on it. Keep the grief. Next year is your turn."

Khalid El-Amin's mother, Arlene, got on the bus when we got to the hotel. She never does that. She had the same message.

"Next year is your turn," she said.

Next year began the day last year ended.

∘　　∘　　∘

It is rare these days to have five returning starters in the college game. Coaches forever have had to deal with the lean year after the good year, a cast of experienced graduating senior champions being replaced by inexperienced underclassmen. That always was part of the sport. The process has been accelerated in the last decade, though, by the Mercedes-Benz lure of the NBA. If a kid can score in double figures and chew Doublemint gum at the same time, he's thinking about the NBA.

"How many kids on my team do you think, in their minds, are convinced they're going to play in the NBA?" I once asked Clark Kellogg, the basketball analyst on CBS.

"Four?" he said. "Five?"

"All of them" was my answer.

There is no disputing the economics. The NBA is the glowing Batman beacon in the sky over Gotham that started kids playing the game in the first place. If the NBA calls, offering more money than I will make in an entire lifetime, plus more than you will make in a lifetime, plus you and you and you, all of us put together, it's pretty hard to resist. The NBA is calling younger and younger players now, feeding the machine as the league expands with more and more teams, and the kids are happily going. Now the college coach might not only lose his graduating seniors; his freshman point guard might become an Atlanta Hawk in the blink of an eye.

We—contrary to the trend—had five returning starters. We hoped.

"You don't have to worry about me," Khalid, my freshman point guard, actually whispered to me after the loss in Greensboro. "I'll be back. A guy just asked me a stupid question about turning pro. Don't worry. I'll be back."

The whispers about Richard Hamilton were quite different.

. . .

Rip was our star. Simple as that. I could hand out the familiar roles to every player in the lineup—Khalid was our motor, pumping out energy; Kevin was our heart, our constant, no matter what happened; Jake was our goaltender, saving all mistakes; Ricky was our captain, steering us away from trouble with his defense, keeping us calm when trouble arose—but Rip would be the one with that star on his dresssing-room door. There would be no argument from anyone on that.

I like having a star on my basketball team. I like having a player available to take the tough shot, to score 28 points when you need 28 points, a kid whom all the other kids can look to when games get close. Reggie Lewis certainly was all of that and more for me at Northeastern. Donyell Marshall and Ray Allen definitely were stars here at UConn. Rip was the next in line.

He reminded me quite a bit of Reggie. He had big hands, a freak of nature that made him different, a true gift for this game. Reggie had long, long arms. Rip probably has a more total game than Reggie, a longer jump shot, more ways to score, but Reggie had that great first step—Michael Jordan called it the best first step he ever saw—and became an All-Star. That's the biggest similarity, I think: that Reggie became an even better player in the pros, and I think Rip eventually will, too.

The idea when he came to us was that he would serve a one-year apprenticeship to Ray, getting familiar with Division I pressure, then take over in the starring role when Ray graduated. The NBA called for Ray, though, at the end of his junior season, same as it had for Donyell, and who was I to argue with anyone over the chance at all that money? (Well, maybe I argued a little.) Ray, after three years, was ready. Donyell really could have used a senior season, but the offer was something like $46 million. He had to go.

Ray's departure made Rip our star from the moment he stepped on campus. He was from Coatesville, Pennsylvania, 6'6", slender, maybe 185 pounds, with a wide, toothy smile. Coatesville is one of those small Pennsylvania textile mill towns where everyone knows everyone else. It is a snapshot out of 1958. Rip is a kid out of 1958. I can't think of any better way to describe him. He is an old-time kid.

His parents are divorced, but no one ever came out of any stronger family situation than the one Rip had when he was growing up. His father and mother both would do anything for him. They are concerned about him 24 hours of every day and give him great direction, great values. He grew up, truly, with direction and love, Ozzie-and-Harriet stuff. The only difference was that Rip senior, Ozzie, and Pam Long, Harriet, lived in different houses.

Rip was a big-time recruit, our second McDonald's All-American after Donyell. Villanova had been another choice, but Villanova brought in Tim Thomas and some other people at his position. That complicated his situation. Temple became a strong option. Other schools surfaced. He strung out the process, trying to figure out what to do. We were involved. We waited.

We don't wait for a lot of kids, but we waited for Rip. He had special status.

* • •

The normal rule pretty much is first come, first served for kids we recruit. We start out with a list of three, four, five, at the most six kids we think can play a certain position at our level. We don't recruit any kid unless we absolutely think he can play for us. We spin our web, lay out our travel brochures for all of them. The kid who commits first is usually the one we take.

The dialogue usually goes something like this:

Me: "We really think you'd fit in well at the university. We think you'd be great with the team we already have. You should sign with us."

Recruit: "If you want me so much, why are you looking at four or five other kids? I know you are. I heard that."

Me: "It's true we're looking at four or five other kids. I also know that you're looking at four or five other schools. Here's the deal: If you stop looking at the other schools, we'll stop looking at the other kids. We can end it all right now. Sign the paper right here with your mom and dad. I'll be a happy man, done with home visits, glad to know that your position will be locked up for the next four years."

It probably is our best closing argument.

Recruiting is an educated art as opposed to an educated science. No one really knows what is going to happen. The recruit probably has the most to say about the situation, but he'd better speak in a hurry. Sometimes someone else moves and a domino effect takes place.

In 1990 we were recruiting Travis Best from Springfield as a point guard. We loved Travis, a kid from right around the corner. He said early that he wasn't going to the University of Massachusetts, so the door was open. I had known his dad, Leo Best, for a long time, since I went to AIC. We were also looking at Kevin Ollie, a point guard from Crenshaw High in Los Angeles. Kevin also was being recruited by the University of Arizona. Travis, in addition to us, was being romanced by Georgia Tech, which also was looking at Corey Alexander, who was a kid from Virginia.

Are you with me? Travis couldn't make up his mind. Kevin could. He signed with us. The dominoes tumbled in a hurry. Travis then signed with Georgia Tech. Corey Alexander signed with Virginia. When the activity stopped, the kid who lived 20 minutes from the Hartford Civic Center was going all the way to Atlanta, Georgia, and the kid from Virginia was going up to Charlottesville, Virginia, and the kid from Los Angeles was going to fly over Arizona and come 3,000 miles to Storrs, Connecticut.

Did any of this make any geographic sense? Everyone wound up happy, I suppose, but . . . geez. Oh, yeah, Arizona went out and signed Damon Stoudemire.

Rip did not have to go through any of this.

We waited.

He signed in April.

He was our star for two years. Now he was leaving.

●   ●   ●

"I hate to tell you this, Coach, but he's gone," Karl Hobbs, my assistant, said. "Believe me, he's gone."

Karl had become good friends, almost family, with Rip. I had to listen to what he said, but I truly hoped he was wrong. Rip, I thought, was not ready for NBA life. I also thought we were not ready for life without Rip.

I had learned long ago that the few weeks immediately after the season ends are not the best time to make decisions. The long schedule, with its day-to-day pressure, takes a psychological bite out of you as well as a physical bite. When the activity stops, usually with a loss and a goal not met, there is nothing. Depression sets in. Every year in early April I would feel sick. Every year I would go to the doctor. Every year he would look at my medical records, see that I had been to his office at the same time for seven straight years, smile, and say, "You're not sick. The season's just over. You're depressed again."

I hoped this was the problem with Rip. The season had been a bear for him. He'd carried much of our offensive load, averaging 21.5 points, 4.4 rebounds, and 2.4 assists per game, taking on the mantle of greatness, Big

East Player of the Year, All-American. He had been bothered by a deep thigh bruise for the first half of the season, an injury that had gone untreated for a week, making it hard to heal by the time he reported the pain. He had the right to feel as gassed as anyone on our team after Greensboro. I was hoping he would get over it.

There was no doubt the pros wanted him. There was no doubt he would go in the first round. The question was where. I worked it out in my head. I figured he would be picked somewhere around 19th, 20th. I also worked it out in my head where he would go in the next year's draft if he stayed at UConn and played at his same high level. I figured he would become a lottery pick, somewhere in the top 10. I figured he would be better off if he stayed with us.

"If you go as a lottery pick, teams have a lot invested in you," I told him. "They're looking for you to make it. If you go as a 19th, 20th pick, move into the league, just shoot the lights out, dazzle everybody, fine. In the second year of your three-year contract, they'll be looking to renegotiate and pay you a fortune. If you don't shoot the lights out right away, though, you might end up forgotten on the end of the bench. Teams don't have that big investment in you. As a lottery pick, you'd almost have insurance that you'd have a chance to play."

I told him that if he thought it was tough here, night after night, wait until he hit that 82-game pro schedule, plus exhibitions and playoffs. There was a happy picture of the NBA he was painting in his head that is not the picture of the NBA that I have. I thought he was being naive. When you go to the NBA you give up all rights, to some degree, to your youth. You can get a nice car and make a lot of money and help your family and do a lot of things, but you're not a kid anymore. Your average social group is now around 28 years old, and you're working a job. I thought Rip was such a nice kid, he deserved one more year of being a kid. I wanted that for him. I also wanted it for us.

In the beginning, I talked so hard to him like this, saying that he wasn't ready, that I just about drove him into the NBA. It was almost my big mistake. One of the things I do with kids, especially the younger ones, is challenge them. I take them down, question their abilities, and ask them to prove me wrong. If a kid like Donyell Marshall gets mad at me, goes out and scores 32 points, picks up nine rebounds, and comes back with a look that says, "Okay, wiseguy, what do you have to say about that?" well, that's fine with me. I've done my job.

By challenging Rip, saying he wasn't ready, I was using my own tactics against myself.

"Not ready?" he was saying to himself. "I'll show this guy who's ready, all right."

His parents were terrific. His mother had done a year's worth of research preparing for this decision. She is an interesting woman. At the same time Rip graduated from high school, she graduated from college. She is the single parent of three sons and was ready to move out of Coatesville to look for a job in a bigger city. Her early choice was Atlanta.

"You don't like me anymore?" Rip asked. "If you're going to move, why don't you move to Connecticut? Then you can come to my games. See me all the time."

She moved to East Hartford with her two younger kids, got an apartment, got a job, started in a master's program, and most weekends came to the dorm room Rip shared with Kevin Freeman and cleaned with a mother's vengeance. She left a different inspirational message on her answering machine every week that was so good, kids on the team would call, hoping she wasn't there, just to hear the message.

Rip is good friends with Kobe Bryant of the Los Angeles Lakers, so she talked to Kobe and his parents. She is friendly with Maurice Cheeks and Magic Johnson, and she talked with them. She knows lawyers in Washington. She talked with them. She talked with Ray Allen and his mom, Flo Allen, who had been through the same type of decision. Her research showed Rip that his NBA possibilities were pretty much what I had said they would be, but she offered no judgments. She told him that the decision was his to make and she would support him in whatever he did.

His father offered a judgment. His father wanted Rip to stay in college, period. He even put the onus on me.

"Why does he want to leave?" Rip senior asked. "Is there some kind of problem with you?"

There was no problem. The one question Rip always asked me was why I didn't treat him the way I had treated Ray Allen. The thing was, he wasn't around when Ray Allen played for me. He would see Ray come back from the Milwaukee Bucks and we would hug each other, kid around, and laugh. We didn't hug, kid, and laugh very much when Ray was on the team, believe me. I treated him pretty much the same way I treated Rip. The same way I treat everybody.

(I've always thought that the players on the team judge you by the way you treat the top two or three guys. Anyone can bat around the last three guys on the bench. That's easy. I think you have to be as hard on the top three guys as the rest. No one should be immune or safe. I do think, though, you have to know who can take it and who can't.)

While Rip considered his decision, I now backed far, far away. I didn't want to push him any more. If I did see him, I was noncommittal, listing the pros and cons of staying in Storrs with the neutrality of a network anchorman. Well, maybe I'd put in an extra pro here and there. Just one.

It became almost comical. We avoided each other. Rip would be inside Gampel, hiding out in the office of Dave Kaplan, our video coordinator, on the lobby level. I would be in my office in the arena level. Josh Nochimson, the team manager and Rip's friend, became the unofficial go-between. He would tell me what Rip was thinking, then go back upstairs and tell Rip what I was thinking. It was like diplomatic negotiations, Washington and Belgrade.

The cease-fire came on May 8.

Rip and Kevin came to my office. We talked for 10 minutes. Rip told me he was going to stay. I think, in the end, the NBA players he talked to convinced him to stay more than anyone else. They, too, told him that it would be much better to be a lottery pick than a pick low in the first round.

He held a press conference the next day. This was such important news that Connecticut's four major television stations broadcast it live, preempting regular programming.

If you think about it, this might have been our most important victory of the season. Five months before the season even began.

.   .   .

We took the kids on a field trip in August. It was a 14-day tour that went from Storrs to London to Israel and back to Storrs. It promised to be sort of like your basic high-school senior trip to Washington, D.C.: a lot of historical sites, a lot of kids yawning and looking for the nearest McDonald's, a lot of worrying about whether the head count would reach the prescribed number when the bus left in the morning. Plus, of course, basketball.

The schedule had us playing six games, international rules, against a string of teams not many people in the United States knew, but good teams, veteran, professional teams that were stuffed with former U.S. college players, teams that could give us serious competition. There was a possibility here for one of those *National Lampoon Summer Vacation* sequels, Chevy Chase in the lead role.

I wanted to make sure that didn't happen.

The NCAA allows schools the opportunity to take a foreign trip every four years, so each kid theoretically can have a travel experience during his time in college. We had never taken one. I'd brought All-Star teams to Finland, Russia, and Argentina, but that was different. We'd talked about doing this for a number of years and finally had put it together.

The funny thing was that we had no idea that we would be taking a great team to Europe. When we'd started planning, two years before, we were in the midst of a troubled season and finished 18–15. We had no idea that the next year's team, young as it was, would go 32–5 and get to the Elite Eight in Greensboro.

Already at least a couple of preseason publications, *The Sporting News* and Dick Vitale's basketball annual, were predicting we would win the national championship. No one was picking us anything lower than third. We were at a completely different level from what we had expected.

Kids, it should be said, are not great fans of these trips. The pictures look great in the media guide, everybody smiling in front of the Eiffel Tower or a pyramid, but if you think about it, the kids are giving up half of their summer, their free time, to do this. We put a load on these kids for the entire school year, and this means the load comes back even sooner. We were together again, first practice for the trip, on August 9.

I'd talked with other coaches about their own foreign excursions with their kids—Rick Majerus had taken his team to Australia a year earlier, for instance—and the opinions were mixed. The big worry is that everyone will get burned out by the experience before the season begins. There is a lot of togetherness for everyone. The positive, though, is that the togetherness also can be very good; everyone is thrown together, with the same problems of food and currency and all the rest, and it can make the team even closer. Not to mention there is a chance to play some good, competitive basketball before everyone else in Division I has even started practice. Who can predict exactly what will happen?

I, of course, was hoping the positive effects of the trip would outweigh any negative ones. I picked England and Israel for a couple of reasons. First, I liked the idea that these were places where English was spoken. Second, we had connections in both countries, people who would help us, especially in Israel, where the legacy of Nadav and Doron has made UConn basketball well known.

I told the kids they would enjoy Piccadilly Circus; they asked if we would have seats close to the elephants. Great stuff. I promised that once we reached Europe there would be no practices outside of day-of-the-game shoot-arounds. There also would be no curfew unless somebody did something really stupid. We practiced for 10 days in Storrs. We were ready to go.

Oh, yeah, one thing.

Our star wasn't going with us.

Rip Hamilton had broken his foot.

He had been invited to try out in Chicago in July for the U.S. team that would be going to the World Championships. It was quite an honor. Only three underclassmen had been invited. The U.S. team was going to be a weird mix of players from the Continental Basketball Association, from Europe, from wherever, sent off in the uniforms of Shaquille O'Neal and Scottie Pippen and other famous names to battle the best national teams from the rest of the world in place of the NBA Dream Team. The labor dispute and lockout loomed over the NBA, and the players' union advised its members not to go to the tournament. This opened the roster for this mix-and-match group of replacements. I thought it would be a great opportunity for Rip to gain experience against some of the best players in the world. I encouraged him to go.

He broke the fifth metatarsal bone in his right foot in the first hour of the first practice, held at the Moody Bible Institute. He had an operation two days after he sustained the injury, and was home in Coatesville on crutches and in a soft cast. I was sick.

Everything was supposed to be fine in the long run, but his basketball summer pretty much was done. Rehabilitation was his summer job. Instead of getting better at the game, he simply had to get better.

His father, Rip senior, already had him on an upper-body workout program that would expand to the entire body when the cast came off. Rip senior is a truck driver who originally was given his nickname for the way he ripped off his diapers as a child, then reinforced it with the way the basketball ripped through the net when he was shooting jumpers as a senior center for Coatesville High. Forty-two years old and a workout freak, he was a good man to have in charge of Rip's rehab.

If there was a good part to the injury, it was that it gave Rip time to be with his grandfather, Edward, Rip senior's father, who was dying from lung cancer. Edward had clippings, starting with Rip's freshman year in high school and going straight to the present, taped to the wall around his television set.

Rip would slide in a cassette of a game he had played and they would watch his style, judge his form. They would talk about life and hopes and expectations. It turned out to be a wonderful, bittersweet summer, the young man from 1958 listening to the older man's wisdom from 1958. The injury seemed to be a blessing.

"I wonder," Rip would say in October, when his grandfather died at age 75, "who's going to put up those new clippings next to the television set?"

He would already have a new tattoo on his arm, honoring his grand-father.

* * *

The British leg of the trip was wonderful for three days. The first stop, indeed, was at a McDonald's, 9 A.M., fresh off the plane. A team demand. We then did all the tourist stuff, sometimes half awake, sometimes animated, as we battled the time change. We watched the changing of the guard at Buckingham Palace, we posed for pictures in front of Big Ben, we went to a session of Parliament. We toured the Tower of London, where I told more than one player that I admired the British medieval approach to discipline and could institute it any day now back home.

Then we played a game. . . .

The trip was not wonderful anymore.

We played at the Crystal Palace as part of the four-team London Towers Tournament. Our opponent in the first game was Rhondorf BBC, from Cologne, Germany. Their coach was Joey Whelton, the onetime mop-topped little guard from East Catholic High School in Manchester who helped take Dee Rowe's UConn team to the Sweet Sixteen in 1976. He had a bunch of Americans on his roster whom we knew, including guards Steve Key of Boston University and Matt Alosa of Providence and New Hampshire, and I said I was worried about asking a bunch of kids coming from the Hard Rock Cafe to play a professional team that had been practicing for a month. I was right.

We were terrible.

We lost, 79–76.

Kevin Freeman had maybe two points.

I was in a funk.

I thought the trip was more important for Kevin than it was for anyone else on the team. I wanted to see some scoring from Albert Mouring, I wanted to see some offensive development from our big men, Jake and Souleymane Wane, but more than anything I wanted to see Kevin play well.

The post-Greensboro depression also had hit him hard. Tied as closely as he was to Rip, roommates, friends, next to each other about 26 hours of every 24-hour day—Kevin had been caught up in the passion of Rip's go-or-stay debate about the NBA. The third member of their group was Monquencio Hardnett, the one graduating scholarship player on the team. Monquencio had tried to live off campus as a senior, giving up his dorm room. When he found, hey, wait a minute, there isn't a cafeteria and there isn't linen service outside the dorms, he tried to get his old room back, but it had already been taken. He moved in as an unofficial third with Rip and Kevin. Now Monquencio was gone and Rip was thinking about going, and Kevin was caught in the middle of it all.

There were rumors that Kevin wanted to transfer, but I never believed them. I thought—I still think—that mostly he wanted to talk with me. He wanted to be wanted.

No kid ever had been a more solid, every-night constant for us than Kevin. He was our grit, our fiber, the backbone of what we did. He was 6'7", 235 pounds, fearless. The picture of him stretched out, saline solution pumped into his body, at the end of the Washington game was a picture that would be repeated again and again as his body cramped, totally spent after a total effort. He gave everything he had in every game he played.

What do you say to someone who does that? Unfortunately, the tendency is to say nothing, to take him for granted. There is the feeling that he knows how much you appreciate what he does and you know how much you appreciate it, so what is there to say? Unfortunately, maybe he *doesn't* know, and that was the case here.

He came to us from Springfield, Massachusetts, a wonderful bonus. He thought about going to UMass, but was caught in one of those Travis Best recruiting dances. There was a kid from Attleboro named Mike Babul who was in the mix, as well as a kid from Kentucky named Dan Langhi.

Everyone played the same position. Kevin was leaning toward UMass, and we had offered a scholarship to Langhi and . . . when the music stopped, Babul went to UMass. Langhi decided to go to Vanderbilt. We wound up with Kevin, and Kevin wound up with us. Thank goodness he did.

He was our presence at power forward. He was big enough to battle big people, fast enough to run the floor. He blocked out; he cleaned up the loose rebounds and put them back in the hoop; he did exactly what he was supposed to do every night. He was as competitive as anyone on our team. His father, Wade, tells a story that when Kevin was in first grade he came home crying because another kid claimed to know how to count to a million. Kevin wanted to count to a million, too.

This was that same kind of competition. He wanted to do more. It was an understandable request. Who wants to spend all of his time on cleanup duty? He felt it might be nice to have a play run for him once in a while. He felt it might be nice to take an actual jump shot once in a while. He wanted to be a more well rounded player. We eventually talked about all of this, and I said what I always say to players who want to do more: If you want to shoot more jump shots, prove to me you can hit the jump shot. It's that simple. I not only wanted Kevin to do more this year, I expected him to do more.

This was his first chance. Rip was gone, too, home, so there were shots available. Kevin, again, had two points.

I was in that funk.

It felt like we'd lost by 30 in the Carrier Dome to Syracuse on a December night. We sent the team back to the hotel and we, the coaches, stayed to scout the second game to see whom we would play in the consolation game. It wound up like one of those torture meetings we have after any big defeat. *What's wrong with Kevin? Are we doing the right thing, looking for more offense, more shots from him? If he doesn't give us the offense, where will we get it? Are there changes we should make? What should they be?*

The next day the sun came out in England for the first time during our stay. We pounded a team from France, Gravelines, 98–77. Kevin scored 25 points, grabbed 13 rebounds. He looked great.

Never mind.

•   •   •

A picture from the Gravelines game: I watched it from a courtside table. I had decided before the trip that each of the assistant coaches would have a chance to coach a game. This was Dave's turn. He ran the bench. I sat at the table, watched, wrote notes to myself on my blue index cards, and stamped my foot at bad moments.

Assistant coaches never get enough credit for all the work they do. Howie Dickenman, that guy I didn't know when I arrived at Storrs, became my right-hand man. He did as much as anyone to build our program in his 10 years with me at UConn before he left in 1996 to become the head coach at Central Connecticut. Dave simply is family. I have known him for three decades.

Karl Hobbs, whom I hired after he served an apprenticeship with Mike Jarvis (that name again) at BU, has become a recruiting wizard. He was a little point guard at Rindge and Latin High School in Cambridge, Massachusetts, teamed with some seven-foot center named Ewing, then played at UConn. He is a coaching star of the future. Tom Moore, breaking down those films, is a new, young strategic mind. He solves whatever Rubik's Cubes other teams might put in front of us on a winter's night.

I wanted each of these guys to have a shot at running the show, making his own substitutions, deciding his own matchups, calling his own time-outs. It was the right thing to do, except . . . remember how you felt when you gave the keys to your kid when he took the family car for the first time?

Joey Whelton came down and sat next to me. He tried to make small talk. I guess I wasn't in a small-talk mood, because afterward he said to the four Connecticut reporters following the team, "Gee, did I do something, say something wrong?" The answer obviously was no. I was just into the game. It might have seemed like a nothing game in the middle of nowhere, but my idea is if everyone is wearing uniforms and referees are present and the scoreboard is working, well, it means something.

I often am asked about my emotions on the bench. People see me chewing my gum at hyper speed, walking back and forth, maybe saying a forceful word or two, and wonder if that's how I am all of the time. That answer, of course, also is no. I put it this way . . . say you're a salesman, a businessman of some kind, anything, actually. A basketball game is two hours long. We play, perhaps, 36 games in a season. That's 72 hours. Suppose you had to make all of your sales, do all of your deals, whatever, in a 72-hour time period. Suppose your entire year were concentrated into that time period. What do you think you'd look like?

Sorry, Joey. Wrong two hours.

* * *

A picture from Heathrow Airport: Antric Klaiber, a senior, the last big man on our bench, arrived for the next leg of the trip, to Tel Aviv, without his passport. He'd left it back at the hotel, which meant he had to miss our flight and take a later flight, joining us in Israel. This was not my favorite moment on the trip.

Antric is our resident problem magnet. If something bad is going to happen, it's probably going to happen with Antric. He had a problem in his freshman year during Spring Weekend, when a party at his dorm was raided by campus police and a beer keg was found in his room. That's Antric. The drinking wasn't even taking place there; it was more like, "The police are coming! Where can we hide the keg? Sure, Antric's room." Many times during his career he had been in the wrong place at the definitely wrong time.

He's just one of those kids. If he's going to miss curfew, he might as well just come and tell us, because we're going to find out. He's a good enough kid, but he has one of those what I call a funny mirror. If I look at him, I see a 6'10", 215-pound, very skilled inside player. Antric looks in the mirror and sees Richard Hamilton. So his picture of himself is distorted. It doesn't truly reflect what the rest of us see.

We all have those mirrors to some degree. When I was walking through the Fort Lauderdale airport not long ago, I ran into a guy I went to high school with. I hadn't seen him in 30 years. His hair was nonexistent on the top. He had a big white beard. He reminded me of the Ancient

Mariner. I said to myself, *This guy looks like he should be a friend of my father.* That's my funny mirror kicking in, isn't it? I'm thinking they must have put me in a bubble for 10 or 20 years to protect me. I can't look like this guy. I'm seeing what I want to see.

Anyway, Antric. I give everyone one mistake. Fine. The second mistake . . . Antric had exceeded the limit. He would notice that a few things were different when we returned from this trip. He would notice that his name had been taken down from his locker and he would be dressing in a separate room with our two walk-on players.

He would notice that, for starters. Yes, he would.

*   *   *

I sat next to former British prime minister Margaret Thatcher in first class on the trip from London. She was going to Tel Aviv to deliver a speech on the Middle East peace process. We were going for four basketball games in 10 days. It all worked out—I didn't ask her about the Falklands. She didn't ask me about the Final Four. Who says I couldn't be a diplomat?

This was my ninth trip to Israel. I have been here more than I've been to any foreign country. I wanted the kids to get a sense of the place, to walk in the steps of history, but also to walk in the political present. It is a different world when two bodyguards are assigned to your team, when a student manager is whisked off the street because a suspicious package has been left on a park bench, when a bomb actually explodes a mile from your Hilton Hotel.

I wanted the kids to talk with the security guards, to know what it is to live in this part of the world. It is a different experience—not threatening, no, not especially, but different.

I wanted the kids to experience that difference.

*   *   *

One immediate fact they learned was that they were celebrities. In the mind of the Israeli sports public, UConn basketball *is* American college basketball. There was a press conference in our hotel. There were stories about us in the newspapers. There were reports on television. This was a big deal.

When both Nadav and Doron played for us, our games were shown on Israeli television. We have had a visibility in Israel now for almost a decade. The talent pool mostly has dried up because the professional leagues have closed the door that allowed players out of the country as amateurs, but UConn and Israel are still linked. The average Israeli probably never has heard of John Wooden and UCLA, Dean Smith and North Carolina, Mike Krzyzewski and Duke, but he knows UConn and Jim Calhoun. That makes it an enlightened country right there.

Our first game, against Maccabi of Tel Aviv, brought us back together with our two most famous Israeli players. Doron and Nadav both play for Maccabi, which is one of the top professional teams in world basketball. Doron is seen almost as the Michael Jordan of Israeli basketball. Nadav, now in his thirties, is a solid player, but nothing like the force he was with us.

Maccabi was a good challenge. It was a better team than any team we would face during the rest of the year. Willie Anderson and Victor Alexander, who both played in the NBA, are terrific. There is a solid Yugoslavian big man and there is also Constantine Popa, 7'4", from Romania, who used to play for Miami in the Big East. Not bad. He was the third-string center for Maccabi. They had size and experience that we wouldn't see anywhere during our season.

We stayed close to them for a while, down nine at the half, but then they wore us down. This was a game where we really could have used Rip. The final score was 91–69. The best part was just seeing Doron and Nadav again. I talk with Doron a lot. He's kind of pragmatic, the way I am, just moving on; I think he and his wife go to India now and study mysticism. Nadav and I also have kept in touch. He comes to the United States every couple of years and stops in Storrs. I go to Israel. We talk on the phone.

An interesting thing happened after the game. Nadav always is calling the office in Storrs, looking for UConn gear. Sweatsuits, shirts, whatever.

The secretaries all love him, handsome guy, the deep voice, and they send him anything. I always thought, hey, he's looking for the free stuff. After the game though, Phil Chardis, one of the reporters covering the trip for the *Manchester Journal Inquirer*, had brought some pictures for Nadav, pictures of Nadav when he played with us. Tears started running down Nadav's face when he saw himself in a UConn uniform.

"I try to tell people over here about these days," he said, "but they never understand. These were the special days of my life."

It all came into focus. He hasn't been looking for the gear because he wanted the gear. He wanted to be linked with us. UConn was still important. I think he's finally admitted that he made a mistake. It only took him 10 years.

○　　○　　○

In Raanana, an exclusive Tel Aviv suburb, we played against Chris Smith, another old friend. After two years with Minnesota in the NBA, after playing in Spain and France and tearing an Achilles tendon and going through rehab, he landed in Israel. I encouraged him to come here. He is only 28. He's still a terrific player.

"Over here, though, I'm just the guy who played with Doron and Gilad Katz," he said.

He said he had received a call earlier in the year from Marcus Cox, one of our recruits, a kid who was going to Kolbe-Cathedral, Chris's school in Bridgeport. He said he had told Cox, who is coming, that UConn was the place to go.

There it was again—the most important recruit in UConn history. The furniture that Howie had bought in a hurry still was paying dividends.

We beat Maccabi Raanana, 75–63 (Chris scored 20 for them), then moved along to Tiberias, a town in the desert near the Lebanese border. This is where war is about one explosion away from happening on any given day. I took a trip to the border—over the border, actually—with Pat, our athletic director, Lew Perkins, and the security guards. You're driving along, then you turn a corner and run into the tanks. It's all cold-war kind of stuff. The signs on the left of the road say Land Mines. The signs on the right also say Land Mines. You can see the craters where missiles have landed.

The gym in Tiberias was actually a gym/bomb shelter, just a mass of concrete. It had the floor of a gym and the ventilation of a bomb shelter. The temperature must have been about a billion degrees. And we played the best game of our year—the entire year—that nobody knows about.

The opponent was Peristeri, a strong, experienced Greek team. This was the first game of a two-day tournament. We played well, but had to hang on just to be trailing by 11 points with about seven minutes left. The Greeks were more physical than we were, and bigger, too. We looked like we were done. And then Khalid just took over. We threw on the press and the Greeks suddenly started throwing the ball away. Every time we had the ball, Khalid made something happen. With 2:38 left we had shrunk the lead to 76–71, and the Greek coach, Argiris Pedoulakis, was kicking his chair almost into the stands. With 21 seconds we had the lead and went from there to an 82–76 win.

The celebration in our locker room was as big as, bigger than, any celebration for a Big East championship. Seriously. The kids knew what they had done. They knew how good the team they had beaten was. The way this game played out . . . down at the half, trailing, then coming back. How many times would we do that during the regular season? This was the foundation. This showed us that we could do it.

It didn't matter that we lost again to Maccabi in the final. This was the important game for us.

*   *   *

I should mention there was a chance to ride a camel in Tiberias. Tourist stuff. I did not ride the camel. The kids rode the camels. Other people in our party—which was about 40 people, by the way, including some Husky fans—rode the camels. I was accused of fearing a loss of dignity by sitting on top of a camel. This was not the truth. I did not want to get bitten by a camel.

One of the stories my father always told me, if you'll remember, was how he got bitten in the butt by a camel in Egypt. He described how the camel simply turned around and took out a nice little chunk of his butt. He showed me the scar. Since then I always have thought of camels as animals who bite you in the butt.

The things your father tells you are the ones that stick, are they not? I remember he always thought Frank Sinatra was a bully. He always said that: Frank Sinatra is a bully, he pushes people around, he's a bully, not nice. I have thought the same way for all of my life. I like the music of Frank Sinatra—who wouldn't?—but if you asked me about Frank Sinatra, I'd say I didn't like him, that he was a bully and pushed people around. I don't know that for a fact, but it's something my father told me, so it has to be right. Doesn't it?

Watch out for camels. They bite you in the butt.

* * *

The final two days in Israel were all tourist stuff. They wound up as the best days of all. I worried that we were hitting the downside, too much traveling, too much togetherness, too much everything, but suddenly the games were finished and the kids were floating in the Dead Sea, splashing each other, amazed at the buoyancy, which could keep an NFL lineman on top of the water, no problem. We were back at the hotel, down at the pool, and the next thing I knew, a manager was in the pool in his clothes, thrown in by Kevin and Antric, and Khalid was throwing one of the security guards in the pool and proclaiming, "I am the man." Suddenly everything was fun again.

We toured Jerusalem on our final day, walked in the steps of Christ. It was amazing to see the effect on the kids. I think people would be surprised to know how many kids on our team are really religious. I bet half of them bring a Bible with them on road trips. To see Ricky Moore put his hands on what is supposed to be the deathbed of Christ, to see our kids walking through the old city, led by a Greek Orthodox bishop, was incredibly moving for me. Religion—probably more so than for most college kids—is a big, big part of these kids' lives.

Khalid and Souleymane, who are both Muslim, followed right along and wound up with a special tour of the Mosque of Omar, from which Muslims believe that Mohammed ascended into heaven. At the Wailing Wall, some of our kids left messages in the cracks in the wall, which is what you do. I think the entire experience brought us closer together. On my part, there was a chance to just sit down with kids and philosophize a little.

I don't know if I would have done that in my first years as a coach. Probably not. We all change as we go along; if you don't grow, you die. That is my understanding of ecology. I think I get closer to the kids now. I think that's my biggest change.

By the time we left, let's see, Kevin had lived up to his new expectations; we'd played a lot of basketball without Rip, our star, and learned not to be dependent on him; we'd won a game that would give us strength during the season; we'd seen old friends; we'd eaten Quarter Pounders and pizza in two different countries; we'd had a religious experience; we hadn't gotten blown up; and Antric remembered to bring his passport to the plane for the return home.

I'd say that was a pretty good trip.

Now we could get serious.

Time to see if we could get to use that key to the city of St. Petersburg.

Chapter 6

19–0

Coach Calhoun,

I went to my first and only UConn basketball game in 1953. At the time I lived on Gurleyville Road. My friends were going, so I tagged along. We got to the Quonset ROTC building and it was sold out. We stood by the door hoping to get in. Someone picked me up and pushed to the door as it was sliding shut. I was the last person in the game and my friends never got in. I had to walk home in the dark.

    I have listened to the games through the years on the radio or TV, missing very few. You have done a wonderful job, but you have caused me to put on 20 pounds this year. You see, the closer the game, the faster I eat. I have eaten salsa, nuts, bread, cake . . . my wife says the dish cloth is missing. . . .

Everett Jewett
Hebron, CT

W e went 19–0 to start the season.

We were ranked No. 1 in the country for 10 weeks.

It wasn't easy.

• • •

The Fitzgerald Field House at the University of Pittsburgh is not my favorite place for us to visit on the best of afternoons. It is a 47-year-old leftover from the basketball times of Chuck Taylor canvas sneakers and little satin shorts and 5-man weaves, cramped and small, a hostile crowd hanging over your shoulder like an angry Greek chorus. The second Saturday in December was definitely not the best of afternoons.

Some needed renovations were being done, which was all well and good, but they certainly hadn't been finished. The visitors' locker room did not have any showers or bathroom facilities. We were told that we had to use a bathroom in an adjacent room and shower across the street. There also did not seem to be any heat in the locker room. The temperature was about 40 degrees.

The crowd was pumped. We were 7–0, No. 1 in the country, and Pitt was 7–3, ranked No. 18. We were coming off a slow-motion struggle against UMass, 59–54, where we did not look very good. An upset certainly was a possibilty.

Possibility? For nearly 40 minutes, it looked like a certainty. We still were learning the lesson of being No. 1—that it is a fat bull's-eye on your chest. The Pitt players were animated, excited, playing as if they were

121

keeping a hostile army from taking control of the student union. They were ahead by five at the half, 13 early in the second quarter, and by four with 10 seconds left.

"Overrated" was the chant we could hear already.

"Overrated."

It was one of the more pleasant comments of the day. From the start of warm-ups, almost two hours before the game, the Pitt students had attacked Khalid. He is an easy target, with his squat body, outgoing nature, Muslim name, and the fact that he is married and has two children. His son, Ishmael, had been born only 10 days earlier. Some character with a megaphone mentioned most of these facts and more. "Fat boy" was a favorite.

With 10 seconds left, though, Albert Mouring hit a great three-pointer for us. He let the shot go as he fell out of bounds, not even able to see if the ball went through the basket. By the time he got back up, we were in a ball game.

We pressured the inbounds pass from Vonteego Cummings, everyone clamping down on a man. When Cummings finally passed the ball, flustered, not wanting a five-second count, his pass went to no one. It sailed over heads and was going out of bounds. Kevin Freeman saved it, despite yells from Khalid and half of our bench to let it go. With an out-of-bounds, we would have had the ball under the basket and a chance to run a play.

"The last two times we'd run set plays like that, we didn't score," Kevin explained later. "I figured if we got the ball right there, we'd run it right back at them and either get a good shot or a foul."

Kevin passed to Albert. Albert passed to Khalid.

Khalid drove into the lane, took a runner, and made it with two seconds left.

Final score: UConn 70, Pitt 69.

The result was mayhem. Khalid jumped on top of the scorers' table to address his surly public. He put a finger in the air, No. 1, and put one of those giant smiles on his face: *How did you like that, folks?* The surly public, stunned, became more surly. Bottles and debris started to fly. Ricky Moore was hit by a plastic bottle that cut his lip. I was hit by a couple of coins. I grabbed Khalid off the table and told him we should walk out with dignity.

"We dodged the bullet," I told the Horde. "We not only dodged the bullet, we caught it and put it in the basket."

Was I upset that Khalid had jumped on the table? Yeah, sure.

But not that upset.

*   *   *

We went 19–0 to start the season.

We were No. 1 in the country for 10 weeks.

Thanks, Khalid.

*   *   *

I never have known anyone exactly like Khalid. I never have had a player exactly like him. He has the energy level of an amusement park ride on a Saturday night in the summer. There is a buzz that comes off him that affects everyone around him, including me. Take a look at him. Listen to him. Can you stifle the urge to follow? He is an irresistible force, twenty-four hours a day.

The shot at Pittsburgh? His life is a succession of buzzer-beaters, everything he does.

"Khalid gets up every morning and drives 100 miles an hour directly to the edge," Ted Taigen, our academic adviser, always says. "The edge of what? The edge of everything. That is where he lives his entire life."

Crisis management is the same as breathing for him. He will finish that term paper, type out the words "The End," at exactly the same time the ball went through the basket in Fitzgerald Field House, the paper landing on the professor's desk as the buzzer sounds. He was married when he was 16, a father when he was 17, a father again this year. He is a full-time student, a big-time basketball player. His religion asks him to pray five times a day. Is this the edge or what? He is 20 years old.

"You could write a great book about his life," says our manager, Josh Nochimson, who lives with Khalid, his wife, Jessica, and Ishmael in an off-campus apartment. "And he's only a sophomore in college."

Khalid is the youngest child in his family. (No surprise there. Have you ever seen anybody who better displays the confidence that goes along with being the baby in the family? Who looks like he's been raised with more love?) He has two brothers and two sisters. One of the sisters is 6'3". His father, Charles, is a bus driver in Minneapolis and an Imam in the local mosque.

Born in Chicago, Charles became a Muslim as a young man, responding to the preachings of Elijah Muhammad and the Nation of Islam. He found that the religion answered questions for him, made sense, gave him direction. He grew to know Elijah, Muhammad Ali, Malcolm X, Louis Farrakhan. When he was asked to move to Minneapolis to spread the word and take over the city's mosque, he didn't hesitate. He has raised his family in Minneapolis.

None of his other kids were big-time athletes, but Charles saw something different in Khalid from the beginning. Khalid pretty much seemed like a basketball prodigy.

"I put up a hoop in the driveway for my two older boys," Charles says. "Khalid was only five years old. The two older boys were playing with the basketball, excited with the new hoop. Khalid came to the back door crying. He said the other boys wouldn't let him play. I finally said, 'Okay,' and I went outside and told the other boys to let Khalid have the ball for a minute. Just to stop him from crying, you know.

"Well, he started dribbling. Not those little pitty-pats. He started dribbling. He'd never touched a basketball in his life. I kept watching him. He tried to shoot, couldn't get the ball halfway to the net, but then he started dribbling again. He had the coordination. I went inside and I told my wife I thought we might have a basketball player on our hands. She didn't believe me. She said Khalid was five years old. He was too little. I said no, he was going to be a basketball player."

"How do you know?" Arlene El-Amin asked her husband.

Charles opened the back door.

"Just take a look at him," Charles said.

The basketball began. By the time Khalid was in fifth grade, Charles was an assistant coach in an AAU program, using his van to drive the Jordan Park Traveling Team to games and tournaments in a five-state area. Khalid played 76 organized basketball games in fifth grade; Charles counted. In sixth grade the number was up to 80, and in seventh grade it was 86. In eighth grade the coach at Minneapolis North High School asked if Khalid could "play up" and join the high-school team. Charles said that was fine. He had worn out three vans on the road trips.

"There wasn't anyone happier to send his child to high school than I was," Charles says. "My wife was ready to divorce me, and I had a new van I wanted to keep for a while."

High school was a succession of triumphs. In Khalid's sophomore year, Minneapolis North won the state title. In his junior year, with Minneapolis North trailing by five with six seconds left against St. Thomas Academy, Khalid hit a three-pointer, stole the inbounds pass, and hit another three-pointer to win the state title. He threw the final three-pointer into the air, watched it swish, and ran straight to the locker room. The highlight was played on SportsCenter around the country. In his senior year, Minneapolis North won the championship yet again, for the third straight year.

I remember somebody showed me a Minneapolis newspaper during this time. There was one of those readers' polls, and the question was, "Who is the greatest high-school basketball player in Minnesota history? Kevin McHale? Or Khalid El-Amin?" I remember thinking, *Gee, Kevin McHale was a pretty good player. What could this kid be like?*

*   *   *

The recruiting worry always is that you don't want to become taken for granted. You like to get involved with kids early, but sometimes the more you're around the more you are seen as part of the wallpaper, a piece of furniture in the living room. We certainly never became part of the wall-paper with Khalid. We were too late for that. The University of Minnesota was the wallpaper.

To tell the truth, we really weren't interested. We thought we were set for point guards. A year earlier we'd added Ricky Moore, and for that year we'd added Monquencio Hardnett. Monquencio was a junior-college All-American with two more years of eligibility, so he had some experience at the position. Ricky was moving into his sophomore year, projected to be a point guard for the long run. So we saw Khalid on an AAU team in the summer and he was playing with Lamar Odom and a kid named Shabazz, who eventually went to Providence, and Khalid was fine, but we really weren't looking at him. We were more interested in Odom and Shabazz.

Then we started playing—it was the 18–15 season—and things started unraveling. Monquencio, it turned out, really wasn't a point guard. He was much better as a No. 2, a shooting guard. Ricky became involved in a situation concerning an airline ticket—more about that later—and was given a five-game suspension by the NCAA. Suddenly we needed a point guard, someone to run the show.

"It was really late," Karl, who recruits most of the guards, says. "I looked around, and the only two kids who hadn't signed—kids who really could step in and help us—were Baron Davis and Khalid. I looked into Baron Davis, but he was a West Coast kid and seemed locked up to a West Coast school. Which happened. He went to UCLA.

"That left Khalid. I didn't think we had a shot there, either. But I was on some trip and I had to change planes at Minneapolis. I bought a copy of the local paper and there was this big column about Khalid, saying how the university shouldn't take him, that he was married and had a kid . . . everything really negative. I called up Coach and I said, 'You know what? I think we may have a chance here.'"

The column and, I guess, the general attitude around the state had made Khalid start looking elsewhere. Here's a kid who had verbally committed to coach Clem Haskins and Minnesota when he was a sophomore in high school. It seemed so certain that he was going to Minnesota that he had a tattoo of the state on his arm. Now even that was part of the negative thinking: *The kid has a tattoo. Must be a bad kid.*

Here's the thing: I don't have a lot of rules. Remember the idea of a quilt instead of a blanket? The more rules you have, the more rules kids will break. You say, well, what happens if a kid is late to a meeting, a practice? The answer is kids aren't late. I think one kid has been late in my entire time at UConn. Kids know they'd better not be late.

I have no problems with tattoos. My son Jeff has two tattoos. Everybody has tattoos these days. I might have liked a tattoo of the state of Connecticut on Khalid's arm instead of Minnesota, but other than that, I had no difficulty with it.

I also had no problem with the fact that he was married and a father. In half the societies of the world, marriage at 16 is a very common thing. Ireland. Go to Ireland—you'll find a bunch of people married at 16. Long ago as it was, I played basketball in college with guys who were married and had kids. You know what? They were the most mature, squared-away guys on the team. I didn't consider the fact Khalid was married as a negative. I thought it was a positive.

So we became involved with him. This was late February, early March. It was ridiculously late to become involved with one of the top 15 players in the country. This never happens. He'd been to Kansas, Georgetown, a few other places, but when I talked to him on the phone, he said, "Give me some time. I've got some things to take care of, but I'm interested." I told him not to commit to anyone until he talked with me.

It wasn't until April—again, ridiculously late—that I visited his home. I sat down with his mom and dad and him. Karl was with me. At this level of player, you're mostly saying the same things all the other coaches are saying, talking about academics and the fact that we're on television so many times and all the rest. Khalid's parents had all the usual questions. I had the usual answers. Khalid was dressed in a warm-up suit. He was going somewhere to play basketball. He hadn't said a word until . . .

"Coach," he said. "Are you bringing me in to back up Ricky Moore?"

I told him no, I wasn't. I told him I wanted him to come to UConn and take control of our team. I told him the way we play, with pressure defense and freedom on offense, UConn would be the best place for him in the country. I said I didn't want him to be our point guard, I wanted him to be a basketball player—and our leader. He listened, thanked me, then got up and left for his game. Karl and I talked to his parents some more.

"We're dead," Karl said when we left the house. "Did you hear that? The kid asked only one question."

"I think we got him," I said. "He asked the only question that he was concerned about. And I gave him the right answer."

He came to campus for his visit, which now has become almost legendary. The kids on the team were playing in the gym. He joined the game. No, he didn't join the game. He reorganized the game. First time on campus. First time he met the kids. He told Rip, Jake, Ricky, and Kevin, all of them, who should be on which side, how many points would win the game, who would have the ball first. And the college kids all listened to this short, stocky high-school kid.

Irresistible force. He signed and said that UConn was his choice because of all the schools he had visited, he thought UConn had the best chance to take him to a national championship. He had—of course—taken the entire recruiting process to the edge and made the latest possible decision.

That's Khalid. The last few minutes always belong to him.

* * *

We went 19–0 to start the season.

We were ranked No. 1 in the nation for 10 weeks.

Nobody even saw some of our best basketball.

* * *

A wonderful thing happened in the middle of our season. Say this was a Tuesday morning in late December, early January. Say the seats at Gampel were empty, maybe a cleanup crew working in the background, that quiet sound of paper cups being swept down stairs, last night's efforts over and done. Say a stranger stumbled through the door. He probably would have rubbed his eyes.

"What's going on here?" he would have asked.

He would have seen a basketball junkie's dream. Flying up and down the floor, full throttle, were the UConn Huskies, No. 1 in the land, working as hard as if the game were being played in Madison Square Garden in front of a packed house. Flying right along in opposition, same pace, sometimes even faster, was this . . . NBA team?

There, in the midst of the action, was Ray Allen, All-Star and now movie star, having played Jesus Shuttlesworth in *He Got Game*. There was Travis Knight, big man, plays with the Lakers and Shaquille O'Neal. There was Donny Marshall and Kevin Ollie and Scott Burrell. Wasn't Scott Burrell last seen kissing Michael Jordan after winning the NBA title? All of these guys were flailing away against Rip and Khalid and Kevin and Ricky and Jake.

This was one of my favorite sights of the year.

The NBA lockout had left all of the league's players on their own for conditioning, maintenance, basketball. Where to play? What to do? These former UConn players had decided to come home.

I don't know if this happened at many other schools—I haven't heard about it if it did—but it happened here, and it was the best tonic you could imagine. Sometimes four of these guys would appear, sometimes one or two, once a week, twice a week perhaps, and practice would become an event. For us, it was like getting ready for a normal Friday-night fight by sparring against Muhammad Ali, Roy Jones, or Sugar Ray Leonard.

We had taken over at No. 1 on December 1, the night we beat Washington, 69–48, in a Greensboro rematch in the Great Eight Classic at the United Center in Chicago. Duke, the early No. 1, had been upset by Cincinnati, 77–75, in the Alaska Shootout a night earlier. We would successfully defend the ranking for over two months.

Early in the stretch, even though we were ranked at the top, I didn't like the way we were playing. There were times of brilliance, but they would be followed by the mundane, the average. Washington was an example, a close game, one point; then we put together a 20–2 run and ran away, 69–48. Michigan State. Same thing. Close game. A run in the second half. A terrific second half. Massachusetts. A slow game. A struggle. Pittsburgh was the low point. The flat-out escape with Khalid's heroics at the end.

I never thought, early on, that we looked like the best team in the country. Duke . . . at the end of the year, Duke would look like a definite No. 1 team, just killing everyone. There were moments when we looked like a machine, but I wanted to see more of those moments.

And then the NBA guys showed up.

We pretty much always had good practices because we had a good second team, because we had a lot of depth. With Rashamel, maybe the toughest guy on the team, and E. J. Harrison, the fastest guy on the team, and with Edmund Saunders and Souleymane and our two big-man redshirts, Justin Brown and Ajou Ajou Deng, there always was a good unit to challenge our starting five. The NBA guys, though, not only kicked up the ability level but brought some excitement.

They went through our different drills, our little practice games, while I kept score in my own quasi-mathematical way, changing the numbers and the rules at any minute to make the drills competitive. (Khalid, of course, argued about every change. He was the only guy on the floor who paid attention to my numbers.) We'd put Ajou with the NBA guys, perhaps, scrimmage and fly.

The kids on our team loved it. What better challenge than to play against someone from the NBA? The interest in practice went up in an instant. You could feel the change in intensity. Right at that midseason swoon, when everybody's sick of looking at each other, exams, Christmas break, the blahs, this was an electric jolt.

And then we started pounding everyone we played.

There was a stretch, starting after the Pittsburgh escape, which made us 8–0, where it didn't matter who we played. The names on the opposition shirts didn't count. Play us and we'll beat you—that was the thinking.

We beat a good Villanova team, 100–76, as if we were playing Quinnipiac. Just another team. We bounced Georgetown, Boston College, Notre Dame. This was the way we could play. This was what we could do. If we could play against Ray Allen and Travis and Scottie and those other guys, we could play against anyone.

Brian Foley, the owner of the Connecticut Pride in Hartford, recently said a silly thing. His team won the Continental Basketball Association title, minor league, and in the euphoria he proclaimed, "We'd beat the University of Connecticut by 60 points." Right. First of all, there is no one close to Ray Allen playing in the CBA, never has been, never will be. The guys who showed up at Gampel would have won the CBA without breaking a sweat. Kevin Ollie, in fact, turned out to be the star for the Pride. Second, maybe Brian Foley should have seen our practices. He would have kept quiet. These practices were not only wars, but close, even wars.

I wish the NBA had a lockout every year.

*   *   *

Exhibit A of how well we were playing during this stretch was our trip to the West Virginia Coliseum in Morgantown on January 9, 1999. We were 12–0. Morgantown is a tough place to play. Again, the fans are on top of you. The spirit of Jerry West roams the corridors. There is a Mountaineer mascot guy who fires off his blunderbuss every time you start to think a coherent thought.

The last time we had gone there, a year before, was the worst nightmare of the season. West Virginia pounded us, 80–62. There was a packed house, national television. No game upset me more during the year than that one.

The stars for West Virginia mostly had graduated, but I was still wound up about the rematch. I wanted to remove last year from my memory. I wanted nothing to do with last year.

"Joe," I said to Joe Sharpe, our trainer, a few days before the game, "where are we staying in Morgantown?"

"Uh, Euro-suites," he said as softly as he could.

"Where?"

"Uh, Euro-suites."

"Euro-suites!" I said. *"Didn't we stay in Euro-suites last year?"*

Joe is our organizer. He started as our trainer in 1995 and was so competent at what he did that I have increased his workload almost yearly. He now takes care of all our travel arrangements, from airplanes to hotels to buses to meals. He is very quiet and always wants to do a good job. He knows that one of my little things—no, I'm not superstitious—is that I never like to stay at a hotel where we stayed before a loss.

"There's, uh, only one other hotel available, the Lakeview Inn, and it's about an hour from the city, and so I put us in . . ."

"Euro-suites!"

I grumbled about the lack of facilities in the boondocks—unlike scenic Storrs—and resigned myself to our fate. This did not mean I had to like it. A man in control never likes to relinquish any control.

Hah. This was only the beginning.

We were supposed to leave from Bradley Airport on Friday afternoon at three. This was not possible because the Pittsburgh airport was closed due to snow. We waited a couple of hours, turned around, and went back to the Marriott in Farmington for the night. The trip took forever, as we were caught in the rush-hour traffic on I-91 and I-84.

The new departure time was 9 A.M. The new problem was fog. We sat in our bus on the tarmac until 12:45, watching the movie *Con Air*. (Why do these kids only want to see movies with bodies falling? The vote for every movie for every trip is for a movie that has a few dozen bodies hitting the ground. The all-time team favorite is *Goodfellas*. These kids would watch *Goodfellas* on every bus trip of the season if they could, especially the part where Joe Pesci puts the bullet in the guy's leg. Could there be something about this too-much-violence-in-the-movies thing? Never on our bus.) We landed in Pittsburgh at 2:30, then took the hour-and-a-half bus trip to Morgantown.

Joe called ahead to the hotel and had our dinner waiting when we got there. Chicken in a hurry. We rolled to the arena, no shoot-around, no routine, no naps, no big chalk talk, two days on a bus, and just throttled West Virginia. From the first play, an alley-oop from Khalid to Jake, foul on the basket, we were rolling to an 80–45 win. It was a complete game, as well as we had played. Rip had 30 points and played great defense as we held West Virginia to 29 percent shooting.

"Call me Mr. Lockup," Rip said.

"How can somebody not score on you?" I asked. "A chair could score 10 points on you."

I suppose you could say after a game like this that planning and worrying, following routine, really are not important. I would prefer to point out that we never did stay overnight at Euro-suites.

•   •   •

We were 19–0 to start the season.

We were No. 1 in the country for 10 weeks.

Life was good.

•   •   •

Christmas came in the middle of the streak. It was the first Christmas where we were ranked at the top. The only other time in school history we had been No. 1 was a one-week stretch in February 1995.

Jim junior and his wife, Jennifer, came in from Beaverton, Oregon, where he worked for Nike. Jeff, who works in Hartford for Smith Barney, was there with Amy, his girlfriend.

"Remember our first Christmas in Storrs?" Pat said. "We were renting and the house was still under construction. We went over there and stayed anyway. We put some lights on an old ficus tree, just to make it seem like the holidays."

It seemed like a long time ago. It seemed like yesterday. In less than a month, against Seton Hall, I would break Hugh Greer's record of 286 wins as a UConn basketball coach. Could that be?

Jimmy and Jennifer had told us before the season began that she was pregnant. The due date was March 17, St. Patrick's Day. Jennifer is a former UConn student basketball manager. She and Jimmy met soon after we arrived on campus, but I always tell him that I knew her first. And I did. She had figured, almost as soon as she heard the news about the baby in the doctor's office, that I would probably not be around for the birth. Something about the Sweet Sixteen that weekend.

Jeff, the reluctant Calhoun when we came here, wound up playing for me. There probably is no one who is more UConn blue and white. He was Donyell Marshall's roommate and redshirted for a year and played for two years before he had to quit due to injuries. His body simply couldn't hold together. His shoulders popped out with every bit of contact. He would go to bed at night and his shoulders would pop out. It was a chronic injury.

"The other kids would ask me about how my dad treated me when I was eight years old, things like that," Jeff says. "They were really interested. I told them it wasn't like the same way he treated me as a player. That's a different thing."

Jeff, I think, still believes that I treated him harder as a player than I treat other kids because he was my son. I don't think so. I think I treated him the same way I treat other players. They all think I treat them harder because of something.

It was a great experience raising both of my sons around basketball. They both came on road trips. Jimmy, who says, "I'm the Northeastern son, the poor one, and Jeff is the rich son, the UConn son," took those bus rides to Orono, Maine, and Durham, New Hampshire, and Utica, New York. I tried to include each of the boys in as many things as possible because the job of head basketball coach is so time-consuming, at least for me, that any shared time is a bonus. They went to the Big East tournament with Pat and me every year, to the NCAAs, to wherever we'd go. They remember playing with Jimmy Valvano's daughters, with Eddie Sutton's sons, on the Nike trips. Jimmy went fishing with Michael Jordan's father. It was a ritual.

"Here come The Calhoun Boys," the great coach Abe Lemons, sort of the Will Rogers of our profession, would say when he saw the three of us. "Back again. The Calhoun Boys."

There are a lot of coaches who work those events, who have little schedules in their pockets of people they want to meet and greet, contacts they want to make in the cocktail lounge or the golf course. That never interested me much. I'd rather be with my family.

．　　．　　．

A visitor during Christmastime, as usual, was Joe McGinn. He was a former UConn manager, a feisty little guy, 26 years old, with red hair and a medical history that could fill about four dozen books. He brought me a fruit basket every year, whether I needed fruit or not.

I met him during the 1989–90 season. Steve Pikiell, who was still playing with us, brought him around. Steve knew him from home in Bristol. Joe was a high-school kid then. He had suffered through a rare kidney disorder since he was three and he was undersized and slowed down physically by it. He'd had a kidney transplant two years earlier that wasn't working really great. He loved two things in life: Boston Red Sox baseball and UConn Huskies basketball.

Five-feet-two, no more than 120 pounds, he somehow invariably had a big smile and a wise mouth. We just hit it off.

"Yeah, Roger Clemens," was the type of thing he'd say. "He's not going to Toronto for the f—— money. He just wants to be a Canadian. Yeah, Bobby Valentine is the guy the Mets need. Yeah, he's a real f—— genius."

We got him into a program at Northeastern, because he'd missed a lot of school with illness and Northeastern had a program for kids in that situation. He went to Northeastern for a couple of years, was a manager there, and everybody loved him, but he finally transferred here. It was his dream. He loved the Huskies. He managed for three years, then, when he graduated, got a job in the graphics department at ESPN. What a place for him to work.

He was in a wheelchair, though, now. Both of his legs had been amputated due to complications with the kidney business. I'd been involved with that, calling him a year earlier from the Final Four in San Antonio, giving him my sad opinions while he was making his decision on the operation. I never treated him with a lot of sympathy; instead I'd say things like "What are you doing in bed? Get out of there." I think he liked that. All he wanted was to be treated as normal, one of the guys. That's how I treated him.

I took the whole team to see him afer the operation. The first thing he did was get all over Rip for thinking about leaving.

"You're going to go hardship?" Joe said. "What kind of hardship do you have? Be a Husky."

He couldn't get out of the car now with the fruit basket, so I went outside to talk with him in the driveway. He was overjoyed at the way the season was going and said he'd see us the rest of the way in Storrs and Hartford and at the Big East tournament.

"And we'll stick it to that Mike Jarvis at St. John's," he said, maybe with a modifier or two. "Another genius in New York."

* * *

The national media started arriving around this time, too. *Sports Illustrated.* The *Los Angeles Times.* The *New York Times.* The *Cleveland Plain Dealer.* The UConn women's basketball team, it should be noted, also was undefeated and ranked No. 1 in the country. There was an easy story here, this up-from-nowhere school in this little town, now the absolute, all-gender basketball capital of the country.

Oh, yeah, and there was the other angle: Why didn't Jim Calhoun, the men's coach, get along with Geno Auriemma, the women's coach? What was the deal?

Read my lips:

I don't hate Geno Auriemma.

I don't hate women's basketball.

I explained, more than once, that Geno and I are not best friends, but I work in a place where I am not best friends with a lot of people. Most people, actually. I don't think I had a long conversation with the football coach, Skip Holtz, more than six times when he was here. I'm an older guy, expecting my first grandchild. Geno's a younger guy with kids in Little League. We're at different stages of life. We both work hard at our respective jobs. We both have had success. We speak in the hall if we meet. We respect each other.

The only problem—I've said this and Geno's said this, too—is when people make comparisons between our two teams, the two programs. There is an unfairness either way. A bumper sticker appeared around campus after the women went 35–0 in 1995 that read UConn Basketball—Where Men Are Men and Women Are Champions. Did I like this? No. Did I like it when people on talk shows would say, "Calhoun should put Rebecca Lobo on the men's team in place of Travis Knight at center"? No. That was stupid. Does Geno like it when other people say, "The women don't jump and dunk like the men, so it's not real basketball"? No.

I think the public saw it all sometimes as just UConn basketball, one entity, interlocked. I suppose that's only natural. I guess I saw more separation between the two programs than some of the public did, more like two separate sports.

I certainly saw the women all the time. They would be in the trainers' room when I did my daily workouts on the machines. I'd hear them talk about their season and their lives. I certainly hoped they did well. The players on their team and the players on our team had some interaction, hooting at each other the way kids do. In the past there had been some dates, a little romance between certain players, but I don't think that was taking place this year. Anyway, it all seemed to work.

At the end of the *Sports Illustrated* article, I said that if I had a daughter or knew a girl who wanted to play college basketball, I would send her to UConn to play for Geno, because there's no place better. Geno said he loved the way my teams played, loved to watch them in action.

"So you said you'd send your daughter to play for Geno," a friend of mine said after he read the article. "And Geno said he loved the way your teams played. And you're both supposed to hate each other?"

We don't. End of story.

•   •   •

We were 19–0 to start the season.

We were No. 1 in the country for 10 weeks.

Thank you, Ricky. Thank you, Rash.

•   •   •

The leader on the floor clearly was Khalid, directing everybody around as if he were the basketball grandson of Cecil B. De Mille, but the leaders off the court were Ricky Moore and Rashamel Jones. There was no doubt about that. They were our co-captains for the third straight year, both seniors, and they made my life immeasurably easier.

It wasn't so much what they did as what they didn't do. They never bitched. They never complained. They never rocked our smooth-sailing boat.

"You've got something to say?" I could ask any other kid on the team. "Look at Rash. Here's a guy who averaged 13 points a game as a sophomore, second-leading scorer on the team. Look at what he's giving up for us.

"You've got something to say?" I could ask again. "Look at Ricky. Outplayed Allen Iverson as a freshman, dusted him for 14 points in the Big East Championship game at Madison Square Garden. Does he complain about not getting the ball enough? He goes out, plays defense. Doesn't say a word."

The addition of Khalid, remember, meant that there would be changes in our lineup in the 1998 season. Khalid's one question—"Am I going to back up Ricky Moore?"—and my flat-out negative answer changed the makeup of our starting five in an instant. Something, well, someone, had to give. That was either Ricky or Rash. Both, actually.

I remember I called Ricky into my office after we signed Khalid. I explained the situation. Ricky was going to have to move to the No. 2 guard from the point. He would be in competition with Rash for minutes. I didn't know how the competition would turn out.

The meeting was for my own peace of mind as much as his. I really didn't have to explain anything, and probably 10 years ago I wouldn't have. I simply would have made the move. My idea always has been that once a kid signs as a recruit, he's giving his career to me. I will make the decisions, based on what's best for the team, and everybody will live with them. If someone doesn't like them, well, he either has to make me change my mind or he has to figure out his alternatives. I felt, though, with Ricky, that I owed him an explanation. He's been such a good kid for us. I didn't have to explain, but at the same time I did. Know what I mean?

I remember his reaction.

"Well, Rash is going to have to sit," he said. "It's too bad for Rash, but if it's between him and me, I'm going to be the one who takes the job."

I can't tell you how many times I've had conversations like this in my office, kids making promise after promise, about how they're going to do this or that, make these or those changes. I can't tell you how small the percentage is of kids who actually carry through on what they say. Talk is so much easier than action over a long period of time. It's a hard thing to do, to live up to your words.

Ricky did.

. . .

Ricky is from Augusta, Georgia. It has been written all over the place now about how he played basketball in high school with William Avery, the point guard from Duke, how they grew up close to each other. His father, Buck, the other story, used to work a regular job and caddied at the Masters every year, then at age 40 decided to caddy full time and went off on the PGA tour. It is interesting stuff. Ricky was nationally ranked as a top-40 scholastic player, averaging 22 points, 9 rebounds, 8 assists, and 3 steals a game.

Anyway, we recruited him and he was interested, but he had trouble making plans to come up and look at the school. There is a national early signing day sometime in November, but Ricky still hadn't made the visit. The signing day was a Friday. He was supposed to come on Saturday.

"Here's what we'll do," I suggested. "We'll write out the letter of intent. You sign it on Friday. Have your parents sign it on Friday. Everything is dated, witnessed. You leave the letter with your parents in Augusta and come to visit on Saturday. If you like what you see, like the way you feel, want to come, you call your parents and tell them to send the letter. If you don't like it, you just tell them to rip up the letter."

It was all legal. The check is in the mail. The point guard is in the mail.

He backed up Doron at the point as a freshman. He had that great, great game against Georgetown in the Big East finals. It was a big comeback for us, a 75–74 win at the end. He came off the bench, wearing a harness because his shoulder had been separated, and put the clamps on Iverson, scoring 14 points. There were, I think, seven players on the floor that game who would go on to play professional basketball—Iverson, Othella Harrington, Travis, Ray, a couple of others. Ricky was the best player out there that night. No argument. When we lost to Mississippi State in the Sweet Sixteen, I think the main reason was that Ricky couldn't play. His shoulder had popped out again in the first round against Colgate.

His sophomore year was just a mess. It was the 18–15 season. We were going along okay, 11–3, and certainly would have finished better than we did, when all this business about airline tickets and an agent came up. A story was growing in Hartford about this guy, John Lounsberry, who had given assorted gifts to Marcus Camby of UMass, trying to build a relationship that would lead him to represent Marcus when Marcus turned pro. The story touched us when Flo Allen, Ray's mother, showed up and told us that Lounsberry had given a beeper once to Ray and had talked with other kids on our team. We had to investigate.

Question: "Ricky, did this guy ever give you anything?"

Answer: "Yeah, he gave me a plane ticket to go home to Augusta when I was a freshman. First month I was here."

Ricky never tried to hide anything. When he took the ticket, he didn't even know he was doing something wrong. We reported him to the NCAA and we also reported Kirk King, our senior big man, who also took a ticket to go home. There were some wonderful headlines—one, I remember, questioned whether UConn was becoming tainted—and it all stunk. Wait a minute, didn't we report all this? Didn't we turn ourselves in? That never seemed to matter. The NCAA suspended Ricky for five games and Kirk King for the rest of the season, which meant the rest of his career. It all stunk.

Ricky had to battle through that and an assortment of injuries. He had nose surgery in November of the season and hand surgery in April, with a concussion and a sprained ankle in between. Then we picked up Khalid for the next season and he had to battle all over again for a job. Even this year, when we went to England and Israel, one of our big questions was about Ricky. Ricky and Rash. Who would play? How much? He had to do it all over again.

He never complained.

That was the thing.

I never have asked him about this, but I've always felt that the embarrassment of his sophomore year, the suspension, the bad press, gave him a fire to show everybody they were wrong. He wanted to make up for all of that. He did anything we asked of him, did it better than we ever expected. He became the best defensive player I've ever coached, and I've coached for 27 years.

Rash, the odd man out two straight years, accepted everything with a grace and silence that I don't think I myself ever could have had. Think about it. You score 13 points a game as a sophomore, second on the team, playing in the Big East, as tough a conference as you can find. You know you can play. The next two years, you average 4.4 and 3.5 points. There are a bunch of games where you don't even score.

It had to be so hard for him. Here was a kid, both Connecticut and New England Player of the Year at Trinity Catholic in Stamford. A local star. How many people were asking what was the matter? There was nothing the matter. I could say things like he didn't put the ball on the floor so well, wasn't able to overpower people the same way he did in high school because at 6'5", 205, he ran into bigger people now, but those aren't fair explanations. He still is a very good basketball player. He could go to Europe tomorrow (and maybe he will) and make money for the next 10 years playing basketball. He could have started for a bunch of teams in our league.

He got caught in a situation where he was playing for the best team in the country. There simply were players who were better than he. Which would you rather be, a starter on a so-so team or sixth or seventh man on the best team in the country? It's a tough decision. Rash came out every day and was a practice demon. He was a presence in our locker room, strong and powerful. The other kids always said he had "a prison body," he was so well built. He never objected to what was happening to him. Not once.

"I know this is lousy," I'd say to him. "I know how you have to feel."

"That's okay," he said.

"No, really," I would say, feeling guilty. "Let's talk about it."

"It's okay," he said.

He would kind of change the subject. Which was fine.

He helped make us a team. Just by the way he was.

*　　*　　*

We were 19–0 to start the season.

We were No. 1 in the country for 10 weeks.

Uh-oh.

*　　*　　*

The 19th game of the season was against St. John's on a Saturday afternoon and was nationally televised. At the beginning of the year, looking at the schedule, it had seemed like it would be an interesting afternoon. Hah. It had become a midwinter heavyweight championship fight, Holyfield and Tyson, 15 rounds. College basketball interest was back in New York City.

My old adversary/assistant/colleague, Mike Jarvis, had taken the St. John's job in the off-season, coming from a long string of successes at George Washington, and had worked some nice magic. Still dapper, energetic, with that tidy goatee and balding head, he had whipped the dormant Red Storm into fighting shape. They were ranked ninth in the country, with a 17–4 record. They had won five of their last six, the only loss a 92–88 thriller in overtime to Duke a week earlier in the Garden. We'd shown a touch of vulnerability, trailing at the half in each of our last three wins, escaping in Miami by a bucket when a freshman kid named John Salmons had his three-point attempt roll out at the buzzer.

"This is a hump game," I told our kids. "This will get us over the hump to the end of the season."

The New York press—which pretty much means the national press—had fallen in love with the running, pressing Storm, anointing St. John's, Ron Artest and Bootsy Thornton and Erick Barkley and the rest, as the probable inheritors of the Big East kingdom, ready to take a few baby steps over the threshold to the top. The baby steps, of course, had to come over our dead bodies. Set up this kind of atmosphere, add in a sizable contingent of UConn fans fresh off the Connecticut Turnpike, stir with a bit of hyperbole from the Horde, and you had a pretty good attraction.

Oh, yeah, and there also was the story of Mike and me.

Let's see, we played against each other, AIC against Northeastern. We coached with each other for one season, Mike as the part-time freshman coach when I got to Northeastern. We met again when he was at BU and I was in my first year at UConn. (Remember the bus accident game?) We bumped against each other a little bit in recruiting while he was at GW. Now we were face-to-face one more time.

I would say we've mellowed in our relationship through the years. We both were assistants to Roy Williams with an Under-22 All-Star team and had a chance to get to know each other better. We certainly respect each other. Mike is obviously a terrific coach. It's just interesting how we keep winding up in these situations. He describes us as "rivals." I'd agree. That's not a bad thing, really. It's actually kind of fun. That's sports. Rivalries.

The game turned out really weird, a game of spurts for each side. If you'd checked with me 10 different times for a reaction to what I was watching, I'd probably have given you five different smiles and five different frowns in the course of the afternoon. We went up 16–3 to start the game. (Big smile.) We squandered the lead in a heartbeat, St. John's tying the game at 22–22. (Big frown.) We trailed at the half, 43–38 (frown), and trailed 53–41 with 17:02 left in the second half. (Bigger frown. I called a time-out and didn't say a word. We knew what we were supposed to do. We just weren't doing it.) Then we went on 10–0 and 11–0 runs (smile) to pull out the win, 78–74. (Biggest smile.) I liked our defense a lot in the second half, holding the Storm to 30 percent shooting.

It was a big, big win.

We all felt pretty good about ourselves. Rightfully so. We were 19–0 and the only unbeaten team in the country.

Rip had tacked a picture of Michael Jordan over his locker, a new ritual. He said he'd read Jordan's book, in which Jordan said Madison Square Garden was the best place of all to play basketball, "basketball world." The picture was Rip's inspiration. He said he was going to take it with him wherever he played. This was not a bad idea. He'd played like Michael Jordan, 22 points, 8 of 17 from the floor. I remember he asked permission to drive home with his mom, which was fine. The rest of us took the bus up I-95. I remember stopping at McDonald's at a rest area on the way and talking with Jake as he got off the bus. He just sort of hopped off the bus, easy, and went into the restaurant. It was all great.

It all fell apart in the next 24 hours.

Chapter 7

THE BUMP

Dear Coach Calhoun,

I lived in Connecticut until I married and moved to New Jersey. . . . I am a teacher and this year I have been using UConn stats for math problems, writing prompts, and just a lesson in loyalty and devotion to a team. . . .

I now have a newfound companion at school who is teaching next door as a replacement for maternity leave. She graduated from UConn in '92 with Scott Burrell. We have shared our passion and commitment for our great Huskies, who have made us so proud, no matter what the NCAA tournament might bring. . . . It has been difficult to tune stations that carry the game into our classroom, while at the same time teaching the children math. . . .

Darlene Biasi
Oakhurst, New Jersey

Jake Voskuhl's dad has the right idea about sports. He's a big guy, Joe Voskuhl, and he was a good player at the University of Tulsa in the early seventies. A rebounder. A starting center. In his senior year, his Tulsa team lost to Memphis State in the Missouri Valley Conference finals in triple overtime, and that was the Memphis State team with Larry Finch and Larry Kenon that went all the way to the NCAA final against Bill Walton and UCLA. Joe Voskuhl knows sports, and he knows how to treat kids in sports.

He says he didn't always know.

"My oldest son, Justin, just didn't care about athletics," Joe says. "It tore me up. This was back when Justin was in grammar school, seven or eight years old. I had been an athlete, and I really wanted my kids to be athletes. The idea that my son was indifferent, couldn't care less, drove me crazy. I made him play sports, hoping he would come around."

One weekend in the fall, Joe was watching Justin's soccer game. Justin, a bad player, had landed on a good team, a team that simply overpowered eveybody else. On this day, the same thing was happening. The score was 13–0 or something. Justin wasn't playing while the lead was built. Put in near the end of the game, only under one of those everybody-plays rules, he was inserted into the goal.

Joe watched and Justin's team continued to dominate, but suddenly the other side had a breakout. The action came toward Justin in a ball of dust, the way kids' soccer games seem to go. Justin seemed prepared for the moment.

Just then a flock of geese flew overhead. Justin's head turned upward.

He was staring at the geese, admiring their grace and beauty. He never even noticed the goal—the only goal the other team would score—go flying into his net. Joe shook his head in disgust.

"It really bothered me," Joe says. "I went to work the next day really dejected. I told some guys that I didn't know what I was going to do with Justin. One guy—I remember this so well—said, 'So what? He doesn't like sports. Big deal. There'll be something else he'll like, something he'll do very well. Your job as a parent isn't trying to make your kids like what you like. It's to find out what they like and help them with it.'

"It was one of those times when you get advice and know in a minute it's true. I've never worried about my kids and sports since. Each one of them has his own particular talent. I try to help each of them succeed."

I wish every parent in the country could be like Joe Voskuhl. I wish every parent could be like my own dad, standing behind center field, just watching and enjoying the game. I see so much of it, the shouting, the pushing, parents trying to live out their own failed expectations through their kids. I call those parents "wack jobs." There are more wack jobs out there than you know. Lighten up. Relax. It would be great to play Division I basketball, great to play center field for the Red Sox, but it's great to do about a billion things. There's something for everybody to do.

"Justin's 26 now," Joe says. "He's an environmental engineer. He's great. My youngest son, Jared, also dropped out of sports. He's a great singer. He's great at Bible competitions. I'm real proud of both of these boys."

He also is proud of his middle son, the athlete. I am, too.

     •   •   •

There is a giant AAU tournament in July every year in Las Vegas. Maybe 250 teams are entered. You can go to games from nine in the morning until midnight. You can see one kid play two or three times a day if you want. It's impossible to see all the games—Billings, Montana, versus Fargo, North Dakota? Maybe we'll skip that one—but virtually every Division I coaching staff is on the case. It's a recruiter's showcase.

I was out there with Karl, looking for kids, in 1995. We went to one of the big-time games, two teams filled with athletes. There were some spectacular players, everybody flying up and down the floor, the game above the rim. Nine of the 10 players on the court were black.

"Hey," Karl said after a while, "check out the white kid. Is he doing as many good things as I think he is?"

That was Jake. He was the unspectacular 6'11" kid with the blond, teenaged haircut in the middle of the spectacular environment. He was boxing out and getting the quiet rebound. Or maybe just keeping his man from getting to the board so someone else could get the rebound. He wasn't scoring a lot, but he was setting screens. He wasn't rejecting a lot of shots, but he was causing a lot of people to go in other directions. He was exactly the type of big man I was looking to find.

It might have been the smoothest recruiting job in history. I don't know if I ever have had an easier time selling the school than I did with Jake and his parents in their home in Katy, Texas. Do you know how sometimes you talk to people and you can tell they're really listening, that they like what you say? This was one of those conversations that simply clicked. I could tell from the beginning that this was going to go well.

Jake had played on a team in Houston, Strake Jesuit College Prep, that had won four consecutive state championsips with a total record of 105–15. He was being recruited by Purdue and Oklahoma State, Rice and Arizona and Missouri, but he liked the idea of UConn from the beginning. He came for his visit and signed his letter of intent in the car on the way back to the airport. He called his parents on the cell phone to let them know what he was doing.

They sent him back to us early, the next summer, to take a course and get acclimated to this new college life in this new part of the country. Here was the picture when he showed up: He was driving a big white truck with the largest tires I ever have seen. It was one of those trucks where you need stairs to get to the door. He was wearing a 10-gallon hat. Was this a young man with a self-confidence problem or what? Six-feet-11 with a 10-gallon hat? Here was a kid trying to be noticed, who didn't realize he already was.

I always say he was somewhere between a Boy Scout and Eddie Haskell when he came to us. He was young. People forget how young these kids are. They're mostly 18 years old when they get here, college freshmen. There probably were 3,000 kids on the campus exactly like him, but nobody noticed because none of them were in the bright lights. Jake, well, you noticed him. I think he set a school record for parking tickets that year with the white truck. There was something about a threat that the truck would be impounded.

For us, he was a different type of kid because he came from a different type of background, a background of affluence. Doron, maybe, was the last kid we'd had like that. I think it caused a few problems. People ask about black kids and white kids on a team, but I don't think that's nearly as big a factor as abundance. If one kid has more and another kid has less, there's an obvious situation. Jake has a godfather, great guy, no kids, who just gives him gifts, anything he needs. Most of our kids don't have that. I talked with Jake after he showed up with maybe his third new winter coat that year and I said, "You know, give it a break."

Our kids are together so much of the time—we have meals brought into Gampel afer practice, then we have study halls—that we have what we call "forced friendships." You'd better all get along, because you're going to be seeing an awful lot of each other every day. There is life inside the circle and life outside the circle. The life inside the circle is the one that takes up the overwhelming majority of your time. It works out. It has to work out.

The thing about Jake, from the beginning, was that he was tough. It didn't matter where he came from, maybe because of his dad, but he was a tough, tough kid. About the eighth game of his freshman year, he was playing against Jahidi White of Georgetown, who was a tank, at least 300 pounds. Jahidi White was just banging Jake, and Jake was just banging back. He was tough from the moment he got here.

In three years he really has grown. Again, that's what college is all about, isn't it? Growth. Those 3,000 other kids also have been growing, I'm sure, but we just haven't been watching them the way we've watched Jake. His girlfriend convinced him to become a devout Christian a year ago and he's really settled down.

I remember as a freshman he was going to quit the team. Which isn't exceptional, by the way. Every kid wants to quit at one time or another. Everybody in the world wants to quit sometimes. I come back to the office after a bad day and check out those money markets every now and then to see how I'm doing, to see when I can get out of here. Everybody does that. Jake did it after the last regular-season game of his freshman year.

The game was at the Civic Center. We lost to Seton Hall, 73–60. It was maybe the worst game any Connecticut team ever has played for me. I was livid. There is an NCAA regulation that you can't practice on the day of a game. So we came back to Gampel and at 12:01, the start of the next day, practice began. How tough was it? For the first hour we never touched a basketball. Ask any of the kids who were there, this was the toughest practice they've ever seen.

Jake went back to his room, called home in tears, and told his mother he was quitting. The whole team was quitting. It was a mutiny. His mother handed the phone to his father.

"Call me back in an hour," Joe said.

The second conversation was less emotional. Jake admitted he probably would stay. Joe told him this was a good idea.

"I can just say this, from playing in Tulsa," Joe said. "If this is the first midnight practice you've had and this is the last game of the season, you're ahead of the game already compared to me."

Jake doesn't score much, 5.5 points per game. He doesn't have the greatest rebounding stats, 6.4 rebounds a game. He doesn't even block that many shots for a guy who is 6'11". In three years, though, he has become as close to being an indispensable player in our lineup as anyone. We're a team, again, that is the sum of its parts, rather than spots of individual brilliance. Jake is a basic part because he frees up rebounds for Kevin, frees up shots for everyone, guards the other team's big guy, changes the game by his presence in the middle. I always call him our goaltender, our last line of defense, stopping the puck after everyone else has failed.

In a game in his sophomore year, I can't remember which one, we were up five with maybe three minutes to go. Jake was on the bench. I called time-out. After I got through talking, Kevin came up to me and said, "Coach, put Jake back in." Khalid said, "We need Jake in there." Ricky said the same thing. They knew. I put Jake back in. It showed how much the kids thought about him.

Now he might be out for the season.

· · ·

Joe Sharpe called that February 1 "The Gloom Day." A fine description. It started with the news in the morning that a bone scan had determined that a couple of stress fractures were running through Jake's left foot. The day ended with our first loss of the season, 59–42, at the Civic Center to Syracuse, an abysmal blowout that surely would cost us our No. 1 ranking.

The middle of the afternoon wasn't much better, either. An MRI showed that Rip had bruised the same right thigh he'd bruised a year ago, almost the same injury. Jake was in a cast and supposed to be gone for at least four weeks. Rip was a question mark. The injury last year took two months to heal. He now was out indefinitely.

Woe is me. I guess it took 13 years, but now I was a true UConn fan as well as coach. The sky was falling.

The news about Jake had started to be bad on Sunday. He complained about soreness in the foot after the St. John's game on Saturday, then talked with our team physician, Jeff Anderson, on Sunday. Dr. Anderson immobilized the foot, said that Jake couldn't practice, probably wouldn't play against Syracuse, and needed to see a specialist and have a bone scan at the UConn Medical Center in Farmington on Monday. Rip also had reported soreness after St. John's, but tried to practice on Sunday.

At about 1:45 on Monday afternoon, having heard but not digested the prognosis on Jake, I ran into Joe Sharpe in the hallway. He, in that nice Euro-suites way of his, had to break the news that Rip couldn't play, either. *Rip couldn't play, either?* Rip had gone for an MRI in Farmington. The test confirmed his injury.

This meant our star, who was our leading scorer, and our top rebounder, who was our goaltender, were out of action at the same time. I had to let all this bad news settle in. After getting past the dumbstruck stage, I began to allow my hopeful side to take a short walk.

Rip, OK, he's had this before. The big problem the last time was that he played for a week before even reporting the pain. The bruise calcified and wouldn't go away. This time, he reported it almost right away. After telling Joe he was having someone massage the thigh and after Joe telling him, "Don't let anyone massage the bruise, it's the worst thing possible, spreading the blood around," he was on a proper course of treatment. He'd miss a game, maybe nothing more. He'd be all right.

Jake? I just didn't believe his injury was as serious as the doctor said it was. The doctor showed me the X rays, good foot and bad foot, the little squiggly lines running through the bad foot. Yes, I could see the little squiggly lines. Yes, I understood. There were no lines in the other foot. What I couldn't do was remove that picture of Jake taking that little hop off the bus at McDonald's on the way home from New York. Would someone with a broken foot be hopping off the bus like that? It didn't compute.

The immediate business, though, was Syracuse. And a sorry business it was. The appearance of Rip and Jake in civilian clothes was a shock to the Civic Center crowd and seemed to be a shock to our team as well. We did not handle this adversity well.

We scored 42 points in the entire game against Syracuse. Edmund Saunders had to hit a three-pointer and dunk in the last two minutes to get us over 40. Forty-two was the lowest number of points any of my UConn teams ever had scored. Thirteen years. Ever.

The reaction of our people off the bench to the situation was terrible. Nobody wanted to shoot. Even our starters didn't want to shoot. We looked tentative, afraid. Ricky wouldn't shoot, Albert Mouring wouldn't shoot. Khalid looked tired. This was the first game Jake had missed in three years, only the second for Rip. Our five-man lineup had been the same for 36 straight games over two years, a 34–2 record, 22–1 in the Big East. I was more distraught about the performances of our players than I was about the injuries.

"Maybe Rip and Jake are the two greatest players in the league," I told the Horde. "Rip is the best player, and Jake stops all penetration, but our other people should be able to stop penetration and make jumpers and go after loose balls and play defense down the stretch. I'm more concerned with the way we didn't play.

"Fate gives opportunites. Right now, I don't know who on our team seized the opportunity."

I had talked with the kids during our 19–0 stretch about this special season, this fragile egg that we were carrying. I told them that if they dropped the egg, it would break and splatter all over. I said I'd seen it happen to other teams. We needed to treasure what we had.

Had we dropped the egg?

.   .   .

Jake went the next day to Houston to get a second opinion from his own doctor. This was a strategy Jake's dad and I had agreed upon. Joe Voskuhl offered to fly his son home and pay for the visit to the doctor. He said Jake had been troubled with foot pain since high school and, from talking to his son, he didn't think the present difficulty was any worse than usual. Joe was optimistic.

I was hoping, too, that the results from this second doctor were going to be great, but in four days we were playing at No. 4 Stanford. This was a game that had been circled on the schedule from the beginning of the year, sort of a transcontinental grudge match. We had tuned Stanford a year ago, 76–56, at Gampel, pounding those guys on national television. They had the same team back. We had the same team back—supposedly. This was their chance at revenge. I couldn't just cross my fingers and hope Jake would be well enough to play.

I had to get us off the canvas. I had to find points to replace Rip, which I thought we could do *if somebody would just shoot the ball.* I wasn't sure what to do about Jake. We hadn't replaced him very well against Syracuse, losing the rebound battle, 37–26.

These were the options:

1. Souleymane
2. Edmund

I couldn't make up my mind.

. . .

Option 1. Souleymane Wane is one of my favorite people. I tell him that. I tell him a lot of other things, too, just about every day, probably with some four-letter emphasis, but I think he knows how I think about him.

No one has gone through more to play Division I basketball than Soule. He is a 6'11", 240-pound guy from Dakar, Senegal, who has forced himself, through his own work and conviction, onto the scene. I can't think of any way else to describe it.

He was at Redemption Christian Academy in Troy, New York, when we became involved with him. Georgetown University has a presence in Senegal, has had a few players from there, and someone had found Soule in Dakar. Soule obviously was a big kid, maybe had played one year of basketball in his life, and had possibilities. A coach arranged for him to come to Redemption Christian Academy. Soule knew maybe one word of English when he arrived. He had left his family, his normal life, and come to America. I think he owned the clothes he wore and not much else.

Redemption Christian is a place out of a novel. It's a small school, run by a Christian order, and everybody has to work to keep the school going. The members of the order and the kids work in a bakery. The kids get up early, bake the bread and cakes and cookies, and then go out and sell them in the area. Then the kids go to class. Then to basketball practice. It is a place where international basketball players go, hoping to catch the eye of someone and stay in America. Charles Dickens would have loved it.

Soule eventually picked up English through classes and watching television. He watched the Black Entertainment Television network a lot.

Me: "How are you, Soule?"

Soule: "Chillin'."

He was so lonely that he would go to bed at eight o'clock at night, just so he could pull up the covers and think about his life in Senegal. He was so determined that he stayed. The basketball did not go well at the beginning. He didn't play much and the Georgetown interest seemed to disappear. Near the end of the season, though, two starters from Venezuela went home and Soule moved into the lineup. Karl spotted him at a tournament in Philadelphia.

"I was in the bathroom after the game," Soule says, describing his first contact with the University of Connecticut. "Karl Hobbs introduced himself to me."

In the bathroom?

"Yes," Soule says. "I was pissing."

His English had improved so much by the end of his time at Redemption that his SAT score came close to the NCAA standard for eligibility. (If the test were administered in French, he'd probably have been a National Merit Scholar finalist.) We advised him to rent an apartment on campus, get a job in Willimantic at Schilberg Integrated Metals, owned by Bernie Schilberg, a friend of mine, and take a Kaplan course for the SATs at night. If he could improve his SATs in time, he could become eligible as early as the next semester. He did all this, working out his own budget, paying his rent, the fee for the Kaplan course, from his salary on the job. This large African man rode a bike to work in the middle of the New England winter.

The problem with Kaplan is that the course is based on raising scores to get some kid a 1,200 to be admitted to Middlebury or somewhere. There was no course that would help a basketball player whose first language was not English get the minimum score he needed to become eligible. Alas, Soule became nervous about the test, and his scores started to go down instead of up.

We decided to bring him in from the cold and redshirt him, admitting him for the second semester, having him sit out the year, then become eligible. This was exactly what happened; he is now in his second season.

Schoolwise he has been terrific, with a major in political science and great grades. I tell him he is going to be the President of Senegal.

I was less certain about his basketball. He has great size, good leaping ability, coordination, but he is about a decade behind an American kid in development of his skills. He is learning the game every day, but starting from behind. We had thought that he would improve a lot this year, starting with the trip to Israel, and become more of an offensive force, but it really hadn't happened. He still was learning.

Could he replace Jake full time instead of part time?

A good question.

He had four points and two rebounds in his chance against Syracuse.

.　　.　　.

Option 2. Edmund Saunders is probably the exact opposite of Soule in basketball development. He is a local kid, from Waterbury, a star in the state of Connecticut from the first day he enrolled at Holy Cross High. Maybe even before that—I first heard about Edmund playing basketball when he was in eighth or ninth grade. He has been raised as an American basketball talent, with all the good and all the bad that goes with the process. He was a great soccer player, too.

If I introduced you to Edmund tomorrow, he would be your favorite kid on the team. He is bright, well spoken, absolutely charming. Of all the kids on the team, he loves college more than any of the others. Not in a bad way. He is the kid who will show up at the drama club play, who will go to the baseball game on a spring afternoon, who is friends with everybody and everybody is friends with him. He is a great kid—90 percent of the time.

Ninety percent is a lot. It is most of the time. He is a great kid.

The other 10 percent he is a mystery.

There is a rage inside Edmund that comes out every once in a while that I don't understand. I don't know where it comes from. I don't know why it's there.

He has had some tragedy in his life. His father died young from colon cancer while Edmund was in high school. His brother is now in prison. The wife of his high-school coach, who was a second father, died suddenly. A lot has happened to Edmund. Maybe that's what makes him angry.

Maybe, too, it is the way great athletes sometimes are treated. He was recruited heavily for high school, with all four high schools in Waterbury after him. Everybody loved him. Then, when things went a little sour, everybody went the other way, labeling him as a bad kid, someone to be careful about, all that stuff. He was caught in that Nancy Kerrigan Syndrome. People seem to want to build up athletes and then take them down.

Edmund, only a sophomore, has a chance to be a terrific basketball player. He's our first forward off the bench, 6'8", 220, gives us depth. He is a great athlete. He is a good basketball player already. He had to sit out his first year because of his academics, but now he was not only playing, but playing better and better.

The rage had surfaced twice on the court. The first time was before the season started, at a practice. He had a fight with Jake. It's interesting, kids don't fight much anymore. When I was playing, there always would be fights, that kind of peacock thing, everybody claiming a piece of turf. This doesn't happen very often now. The attitude is "whatever." I saw it during the Latrell Sprewell business with P. J. Carlesimo. Did you watch the interviews with all the players? Nobody took a side, nobody said one guy was right and one guy was wrong. It was all "whatever." The fight between Edmund and Jake was anything but that.

It started with the usual stuff under the basket, elbows back and forth, and then things got out of hand. It was a serious fight, took a while to break up. All of us were pulling them apart. It all cooled down in the end— I made them shoot foul shots together and they're fine now, friends—but it was scary while it was going on.

The second fight was during our game against Fairfield. That was more understandable. This was one of those cheap-shot games, a million things taking place. Rash was submarined on a fast-break dunk near the end. Everybody got into a tangle. Edmund threw a punch, and he was ejected. The thing was, once you're ejected for fighting during the season, if you get ejected one more time, you're suspended for the rest of the season. Edmund was driving with a black mark on his basketball license.

The big thing with Edmund is making him calm down, helping him learn to say "whatever." He shows up some nights in an emotional fervor. He shows up other nights calm, ready to take care of business. We're looking for the calm. In the Syracuse debacle, he probably was our sole bright light. He was the leading scorer, 14 points, mostly while he was taking Jake's spot.

Could he do that consistently? He would be giving away size most nights as a forward in the middle. Would that help his development or hurt it? Would we simply need Soule's height and bulk against bigger people? Would we have to do this by committee? Could we make serious changes in responsibilities this late in the game and still keep rolling?

*　　*　　*

We never had to find out. Jake was back.

*　　*　　*

The squiggly lines turned out to be old squiggly lines. The little hop off the bus on the way to McDonald's turned out to be a better indicator than the X-ray machine. Jake's physician, Dr. Donald Baxter, a nationally known orthopedic specialist, compared old high-school X rays of Jake's foot with the new X rays from Farmington and said the squiggly lines were exactly the same. His only recommendation was that Jake wear new sneakers every practice and game for extra strength, extra stability.

Jake could play on Saturday.

"All things happen for a reason," Jake's mother, Caren, says now, talking about the injury scare. "The Lord just wanted Jake to come back to Houston. There was something He wanted to take care of."

She tells an amazing story. She went to see the doctor with Jake and his friend Clint Ray. Clint was a teammate of Jake at Strake Jesuit Prep. He was the point guard, the assist leader, a double-digit scorer. He went to San Jacinto Junior College in Texas on a scholarship but had problems with his shinbones. He eventually had surgery, long metal rods inserted in the shinbones of each leg. He tried to return to basketball but found he couldn't play. The metal rods would cut through his skin, wouldn't allow him to run. He had lost the scholarship and was out of school.

Jake and his mother met Clint for Mexican food, then went to the doctor's office. Dr. Baxter examined Jake, then sent him to the waiting room. After examining the X rays, the doctor delivered the happy news. He then looked at Clint. He could see Clint's discomfort.

"What's the deal with you?" Dr. Baxter asked. "What's your problem?"

The doctor examined Clint and said there was a way now to fix his weak shins without the rods. He scheduled surgery, eventually took out the rods, and after a period of rehabilitation and treatment, the shins have healed. Clint Ray is playing basketball again, looking into options for school.

"It's a miracle," Caren Voskuhl, who has become a Christian with her son, says. "If Jake hadn't come home, Clint never would have seen the doctor and the doctor never would have seen Clint."

It sounds good to me.

I thought it was a miracle that Jake was back.

*　　*　　*

The worry now was Rip. Jake greeted us at the airport in California, everybody giving high fives, but Rip still was struggling with his injury. Half of the problem was his thigh. Half of the problem was regaining his confidence.

His recovery from foot surgery in the summer had been slow, the aftereffects lingering into the first third of the season. The memory of his long bout with the similar thigh problem of a year ago was fresh. He still felt pain, and pain told him to stop.

Joe Sharpe told him that the discomfort was natural, that he had to battle through it, that he wouldn't hurt himself any more. In fact, he would get better. Rip was hesitant. I think he was wondering if he were ill-fated or something.

He decided to try the leg on Friday at our practice. You could see he just wasn't right. He fell down twice simply trying to run. He told Joe he felt a stab of pain. Joe told him again that it was all right, that it was the adhesions ripping free. Rip really didn't buy it.

I knew he was out of the lineup.

I'll admit that I got a little nasty. I told the kids that one f—— guy (adjective for emphasis) wasn't going to determine our success. I said we all knew how important Rip was and we all knew how much we loved him, but if he couldn't go, he couldn't go, and, you know what, it didn't make any difference. Stanford was not going to get any quicker between now and Saturday afternoon.

That was the big matchup, our speed against their size. It's a matchup I'll take any day of the week. We had run Stanford silly a year before, and I thought we could do it again, Rip or no Rip. I even played golf after practice to show how confident I was. Hah. I never play golf during the season, much as I love it. Ted Taigen and Tim Tolokan had plotted this for months, however, getting my commitment before the season began to play at the club where Ted's dad belongs. I went, I played. I enjoyed about eight holes, but for the last 10 holes my mind was at Maples Pavilion.

The game was being given one of those War of the Worlds buildups. Stanford had never before been on national network television. ESPN, yes. CBS, ABC, never. Students had started camping out on Thursday for the Saturday game. A poster in the Stanford locker room listed the team's goals for the season, and right under "Win NCAA championship" and "Win PAC-10 title" was "Beat the University of Connecticut. We owe them 40 minutes of hell at Maples—payback time on our turf, with the entire nation watching." This was serious stuff.

"After you get killed by a team like Connecticut, it not only motivates you for right now, it motivates you for over the summer," Stanford big man Mike (Mad Dog) Madsen told our visiting Horde. "I think a lot of us thought about that game in the spring, in the summer, in the autumn—when we were out doing chin drills. You can't erase something like that out of your mind."

I had been doing a little motivating of my own. During the week I'd had a little chat with Mr. El-Amin. I wanted him to get back some of that spirit I thought he'd been lacking.

"Is the fire still in your belly?" I asked him. "Because I've done over 800 of these games and it's still in mine."

"Yeah," Khalid said. "It's still there."

If he needed any other motivation, well, the Stanford students certainly did the job for him. They call themselves the Sixth Man and the only thing they consider sacred is the idea that nothing is sacred. Good taste certainly isn't. They started with "fat boy" and "dough boy" chants and went down to "who's your baby?" and "deadbeat dad." They had signs that read Khalid: One Word—Slim-Fast and a photo of him with a smile and a McDonald's logo over his head. They had a sign that said Another Bastard Child and a sign that said I'm Khalid's Kid next to one that said Me Too. They pretty much covered the subject.

(Item one: Khalid is not fat; he is stocky. We have had his body fat measured and it is well below normal. He simply has a fireplug kind of body. Item two: The names of his two kids are written on his sneakers. He is married and he pays his bills.)

Taken to the edge, well, our man at the edge was his old self. He had 23 points, 5 assists, and 5 steals. We had a 70–59 win, totally as convincing as the previous year's win in Storrs. It was a terrific effort from everyone, a win like we hadn't had for a long time. Cast back in that underdog role for the first time this season, we showed that we liked it. I hadn't felt this good after a win in a long time.

"Look at the scoreboard," Khalid simply said as he left the floor—no trip to the scorer's table this time. "Look at the scoreboard."

"We've had a lot of special victories," I told the press, "but I can't remember too many like this. I'm impressed and, as you know, I don't impress easily."

Kevin Freeman again was a picture of our effort. He battled Madsen elbow for elbow and finished with 14 points, 11 rebounds. Madsen finished with 13 points, 9 rebounds. Kevin was back on the floor in the locker room and again in the aisle on the plane home, getting that saline solution pumped into his body. ("He can't be down there," the flight attendant said. "He can't get up," someone replied.) He even lay on the floor during a time-out during the game, 5:24 remaining, then stood up and resumed the battle.

"How could you seem to be in such pain one minute, then back on the floor in the next?" a member of the Horde asked.

"I was reincarnated," Kevin said.

The whole team was. Sort of.

.   .   .

Our occupancy of the No. 1 spot officially ended the morning after the Stanford win as the weekly rankings came out. Duke ascended to the throne, rightfully so, unbeaten since that early-season loss to Cincinnati in Alaska.

I'm not a great believer in the polls. I'm more concerned with what my eyes tell me, whether I think we're playing well or not well. In this case, though, the polls had it right. They saw the same thing I saw. Duke was cruising. We had some work to do.

I'd made it a point to find Rip after the Stanford game. I told him that I'd just congratulated the kids on their great win, which it was, but that I knew it was a one-day deal. We couldn't do that every day. We needed him.

He came back the next game against Boston College, a 66–50 win, and was just painful to watch. He was 4 for 15 from the floor, with 9 points, and just stood around a lot. Think about his situation: He was a first-team All-American, he was a candidate for Player of the Year, and he was struggling. He had no confidence in his leg and probably didn't have any reason to have confidence. The first game we played against Boston College, in Boston, he scored 39 points. Now every basket was like it was squeezed out of a tube of toothpaste that's nearly empty, the bottom all rolled up, heavy pressure needed for even the smallest result.

This was something that Rip—and we—had to get through. He struggled again against Seton Hall and against Rutgers. We simply had to wait it out. Jake was struggling, too. He limped off the court two minutes into the second half against Rutgers and didn't return. He'd practiced five days in a row before the game, and the work obviously didn't agree with him. I didn't want him to be a game-only player, but I also didn't want him to be sidelined for the season. Joe and Jake and I worked out a schedule that would give him rest some days but allow him to practice on other days.

We were still carrying that egg, but we looked a little like Charlie Chaplin in the middle of traffic, maybe Buster Keaton on a scaffold, while we were doing it. And the University of Miami didn't help.

● ● ●

I do respond to the negative. Yes, I do. I once heard a quote from a member of the Horde where the guy said he always rooted for UConn to lose because the stories were better because I invariably had more interesting things to say after a loss. Well, he got his wish against Miami. I just don't know how many interesting things I had to say.

Miami was like the new contender in the WBA-WBC boxing ratings, the tough kid from the barrio, full of determination, ready to knock out the wily old champ. We had a chance to clinch the Big East championship on this final Saturday afternoon at Gampel, Senior Day, with all the awards and ovations for Ricky, Rash, E.J., and, yes, Antric before the game. The Hurricanes, trailing by two games, had a chance to extend the race through our final two road trips to Providence and Syracuse. Well, it was not a pleasant sight, the wily old champ stretched out on the canvas at the end, wondering what had hit him.

There could have been an escape, Khalid didn't see a pass to an open Rip and wound up missing a 17-footer as the horn sounded for the 73–71 finish, but this was a game we squandered 73 different ways. How can we look so flat-out brilliant at times and then ordinary at others? We should have wrapped this up in the first half when we sailed to a 10-point lead, then 14. We became overconfident and cocky, and we lost our zip. We just let the game get away. There was no help from the bench. We were killed in offensive rebounds. Nobody could throw a simple pass except Ricky. Our only offense at the end seemed to be jumpers from Rip and Khalid, nothing else.

I fed the Horde as best I could, going into a defensive mode.

"I wouldn't want my team at 23–2 to think they're having a bad year," I said. "Some of you might want to write that, think that, or feel that. I'm not saying you do, but it does make better copy. I know."

I then went into a meeting.

We had not had an all-out torture meeting since, well, our three-point win over Marathon Oil in the first exhibition game of the year, when Dave and Karl and Tom and I started talking and didn't leave Gampel until four or five in the morning. (Did it work? I don't know. We did go 19–0 to start the season.) This, to me, was a good time for another meeting.

I suppose whatever we all had to say, whatever change we wanted to make, could have been decided in 45 minutes, maybe less, but I like the idea of closing the door in times of stress, taking a situation, and attacking it from as many different directions as possible, again and again—not only beating a dead horse, but waiting until it decomposes. I know it drives my assistants crazy. Howie Dickenman, now the head coach at Central Connecticut, used to start doing calisthenics while we talked and talked. Dave lies down on the couch and promises not to close his eyes. Tom, I think, is amazed at it all.

"We'll talk, say, for four or five hours about Ray Allen," Tom once said. "What's wrong with Ray? Why isn't Ray playing better? Does he have some personal problems? Is it something in school, a class? How can we get Ray the ball more? What do we have to do to win? We'll talk half the night away. I'll wake up in the morning and look at the paper, which says that Ray Allen scored 26 points and had 10 rebounds and UConn won by 20. What were we talking about?"

I simply like the way a meeting focuses attention on a problem. It makes the problem important. Sometimes if you talk about something for a few hours, you see it from a different angle; somebody has a different thought. The meeting forces you to think. The meeting shows how important you think this job is.

It all goes back to my belief in hard work: The more productive work you do, the better you will be. I'm kind of a fan of Bill Clinton. He's certainly made some mistakes, has some demons, but I like the way he's worked to get where he is. Nobody ever gave him anything—he came from a tough background, the whole thing. He's probably our first self-made president since . . . I don't know. Harry Truman? Fifty years? You look at the way he became president, going to the Wal-Marts and the luncheonettes in New Hampshire, shaking hands, winning the primary on a person-to-person campaign. Nobody gave him a chance, but he worked hard and did it.

Senator Chris Dodd of Connecticut once told me that Clinton's greatest gift was to turn negatives into positives, that he worked best when things were falling down around him. I can understand that, responding to a challenge. George Stephanopoulos's book tells how Clinton always is bitching about the speeches his writers write for him—nothing is right, everybody making changes until the last moment—then he goes out and gives the speech perfectly. I can understand that, too. I think the common thing with people who succeed is that fear of failure. Fear of failure makes you work.

I have that fear big time. I'm thinking about the team, the games, the practices, every minute I'm awake. I'll have thoughts in the middle of the night: *I should say this to Khalid. I should say that to Kevin.* Managing on emotion, which is a lot of what coaching is, is very difficult. You can react from emotion, but you'd better have some thought behind it.

I try to talk to each kid every day, to say something to him, even if it's just hello. I want them to know how important this is. If I don't talk, well, sometimes silence is even more effective than words. Take Khalid. The worst thing I can do to him is not talk to him. If I walk by him and don't say a word, he'll be in my office in 10 minutes, asking, "What did I do wrong?"

This torture meeting started around 4 in the afternoon. It hadn't been planned, so Pat needed to take the car to get home. I said I'd get a ride with Tim Tolokan, who had to take care of the stats and prepare some press releases. Tim finished his work around seven o'clock and started checking every so often at my office to see if I were ready to leave. Eight o'clock rolled around, then nine. He finally gave up and went home around 9:30. When the meeting broke up, around 11 o'clock, maybe midnight, I called Pat to come and pick me up.

It was a good meeting. We decided what was, I guess, the obvious: We had to get Rip going 100 percent. We had to get Khalid to be more focused during the entire game, not just in the winning time at the end. Basically, we concluded that the UConn basketball Huskies simply had to kick it up, play better.

And guess what? They did.

•   •   •

UConn 72, Providence 65. (Providence Civic Center.)

UConn 70, Syracuse 58. (Carrier Dome.)

End of regular season.

Record: 25–2. Big East standing: first. (Champions for second straight year, fifth of past six years.)

After the Miami loss, someone wrote that "the baton had passed in the Big East from UConn to the Hurricanes."

"I think that baton is being FedExed back," I told the Horde after the Syracuse win. Good for us.

•   •   •

The Big East is our neighborhood, okay? The Big East is where we eat, sleep, bump into people when we buy our groceries. The neighborhood might have expanded in recent years, so that we sometimes go to South Bend, Indiana, and Morgantown for those groceries, but it's still the neighborhood.

Success in the neighborhood, being the best on your block, still is very important to me. If you aren't the best on your own block, then how can you hope to be the best on all the blocks? It seems simple to me.

When I started at UConn, going to the Big East tournament at Madison Square Garden was a crusade. UConn had been humiliated for so many years, eliminated early, often in that old eight-nine game before the tournament really began. The Big East tournament was a major goal. I remember talking to the Horde after my first tournament game in the Garden, when we were eliminated, 61–59, in that dreaded eight-nine matchup. I was kind of emotional. I promised we would never play in that game again. And we never did.

With our successes in recent years—and with the larger question of the NCAAs and that elusive trip to the Final Four always looming—I think our fans and the media began to downplay the importance of the Big East tournament. I never did. I always say that the regular-season championship is more important because it involves more work, more games, and is a more honest test of abilities, but the tournament is also very important. Anything about the Big East, our neighborhood, is important.

That was why I was upset, even before I got to New York.

The various Big East honors for the regular season had been announced. Rip was named Co-Player of the Year, which was great. After all of his injury problems, he became only the third player in the 20-year history of the league to win the award two years in a row, along with Chris Mullin of St. John's and Patrick Ewing of Georgetown. Pretty good company. Khalid, however, had been named only to the second team, All-Conference, which was not great. Excuse me, hadn't anybody been watching?

Ricky, the best defensive player I ever had coached, was not the defensive player of the year? He was my choice.

And—worst of all—Kevin was honored for nothing. His name wasn't in any of the top three All-Star teams in the league.

"We were 25–2, we're ranked No. 3 in the country," I told the Horde. "More than two people contributed to that. At 16–2 in the league, 9–0 on the road, first team in history to do so—somebody must have done something for us. But Pittsburgh [5–13] has as many all-league players as we do. Something's very wrong here."

I felt terrible for Kevin. I told him so.

He'd done everything he'd promised to do when we'd had our talk in the spring, when there were rumors about his leaving. We'd expanded his role, as promised, and he'd more than filled it, as promised. How could he not have been noticed? He was a constant for us, always getting the tough rebound, guarding the tough forward, doing any little dirty job that needed to be done.

He's such a good kid. He's the first kid at study hall every night, the last to leave. The one light still on in the airplane coming home, except for mine, always belonged to Kevin; he'd be studying. In the middle of the season he went through a tough personal situation. For two years he'd thought he was a father. He had been paying child support, helping to raise a little boy he thought was his son. The boy's picture was on his desk in the room he shared with Rip. He loved his son. The boy's mother was looking for an alteration of the support agreement and as part of it went through an obligatory blood test simply to prove that Kevin was indeed the boy's father. To both her and Kev's surprise, the blood test showed that Kevin could not be the boy's biological father.

Kevin, the way he is, was heartbroken. How can you turn off love? Rather than keep all this to himself, he talked about it in the newspapers, detailed his anguish. It was Kevin all the way—the honest workman. He battled through that the same way he battled through Mad Dog Madsen's elbows in Palo Alto. If he couldn't battle anymore, well, stretch him out on the floor and feed him some fluids and he'd get up and battle some more.

As coaches, we always are trying to sell the idea that flash doesn't count, that points and headlines are on the surface, that contributions to the common cause, the collective endeavor, are what are important. How could the league's coaches, who were the ones who had voted for all these awards, have failed to see all that in Kevin?

I told the Horde I was going to propose that the ballot be taken away from the coaches and given to a 39-person media panel, three writers for each team in the league. Maybe the coaches are too busy with their own teams to see what other teams are doing. Maybe the media—terrible as this is to say—can actually see what is taking place during a game better than the coaches.

I was upset.

So was Kevin. That was good.

*　*　*

For three days, he put on a performance that was nothing less than you-can-kiss-my-butt perfect. He saved us from embarrassment in the quarter-finals with 22 points and five rebounds as we came from behind for a 57–56 win over Seton Hall, a team that played us tough in all three meetings during the year. He had 21 more points as the afterburners finally kicked into action for the entire lineup in a 71–50 rout of Syracuse. He was back to being solid old Kevin in the final, nine points, six rebounds, solid everywhere in an 82–63 demolition of St. John's that was never in doubt after we scored the first 13 points of the game.

I thought Rip, in the final two games, looked for the first time like he was fully recovered from his thigh. He was moving without caution, shaking free and just drilling every shot he had. I thought Jake, playing three games in three days, seemed as if he might be able to stay in one piece. He'd missed the final regular-season game in Syracuse with more pain in his foot. I thought our bench, sometimes invisible during the season, looked like it could help. Souleymane was solid. Rashamel gave us some points. Edmund, E.J., even Antric—everyone made me feel good.

I felt best of all about Kevin. Throughout the St. John's win, the UConn fans, who had taken charge of the Garden, chanted "MVP, MVP, MVP" whenever he did something. They knew the story, how he'd been slighted. I've never seen our kids happier when an award was presented. You could just see that it meant something to every one of them when the announcer said, "Most outstanding player in the tournament . . . Kevin Freeman." Rip was all over him, hugging him, punching him.

Take that.

Is it better to be third-team All-Conference or tournament MVP?

I'll go with MVP.

      •   •   •

A picture from the Big East: I became a grandfather before the Syracuse game in the semis. The Horde said "Grumpy" became "Grampy." Very clever, boys. Thank you very much. The baby, Emily, seven pounds, two ounces (and I hope with a coachable disposition), was born 12 days earlier than originally expected in Portland, Oregon, to Jennifer and Jimmy.

Jennifer called from the delivery room as they were stitching her up. She knew what our schedule would be—once a manager for the Huskies, always a manager for the Huskies. The baby was born at 4:21 Eastern time, and she reached me in the lobby of the New York World Trade Center Marriott as we waited for the 4:30 departure of the bus for the game. She and Jim—and sometimes Emily—watched the game in the recovery room. Emily got a little publicity on the ESPN broadcast.

The conventional wisdom is that her birth would make, did make, has made me a mellower individual. I simply don't buy that.

I had a technical in that Syracuse game.

A woman has to learn early to stand up for her rights.

      •   •   •

A second picture from the Big East: The last person in our locker room after the St. John's win was Joe McGinn. He was in his wheelchair in the middle of the room. Ricky hugged him and they exchanged congratulations. A lot of players stopped and talked. I stopped.

"Yeah, Mike Jarvis . . . ," he said. The usual stuff.

Dave was the one who left with him.

"Joe was the last one out of the locker room," Dave told Mike Arace of the *Hartford Courant*. "We talked while he wheeled over to the freight elevator. He was kidding Scottie Burrell about his new girlfriend. We got into the elevator. He wasn't feeling well, but there were plenty of times when we'd seen him not feeling well. When he was 16, he wasn't supposed to make it to 18."

I talked to him the next night after the tournament selection show. Going over the brackets was something we did every year. He liked our bracket for once, going west, seeded No. 1. For once, he said, we hadn't been screwed. He liked our chances. I told him I liked our chances, too.

I never got a chance to talk to him again.

Chapter 8

NCAAS

Dear Coach Calhoun,

I just wanted to take the opportunity to thank you for all that you did for my cousin, Joe McGinn. I know I speak for the rest of the family as well as myself when I say that you and your team will always have a special place in my family's heart as well as mine. What you did shows that you all are not only champions on the court, but especially off the court.

Jon Peyton
Bristol, CT

The chapel at the Air Force Academy is not the best place to begin "The Road to the Final Four," as CBS describes the trip. We were a sad group that listened to Captain Kent Johnson, the Air Force chaplain, deliver a sermon based on the Twenty-third Psalm, about walking into the Shadow of the Valley of Death. Joe McGinn already was there.

The news was waiting for us when we arrived in Denver for the first round of the West Regionals. The little guy had come back from the doctor's office in the morning with a note that said he could return to work. In the afternoon he'd suffered a heart attack in his bed.

"His heart just gave out," his mother, Sheila, said to me. "He'd fought so hard for so long."

He'd been on dialysis four times a day, trying to keep his kidney working. He'd been hooked up to the machine by his friend, Dave Polochanin, in the hotel room just before he came to the St. John's game in New York. It was a hard, hard existence.

"I tried to resuscitate him," Sheila said, "but as I looked at him I knew how his body had been ravaged for so long. It just couldn't take any more."

I told the team the news that night in Ricky's room at the captain's meeting and set up the memorial service for the next day, since we wouldn't be able to attend the funeral. The older players, closer to Joe's age, Rash and Ricky, knew him best. They had been on the team when he was still a manager. But everybody knew him. He was a presence, always outside the locker room in his wheelchair, always with something to say. Seeing Joe was as natural as seeing Jonathan, the school mascot. More natural. Joe was around more.

Captain Johnson didn't know Joe, of course, but he was a former basketball player from Pittsburgh who had played for Marshall. He knew athletics, athletes, the athletic life. I talked with him for 15, 20 minutes, telling him about Joe, and he gave a wonderful sermon. There were maybe 25 of us in this chapel in the middle of the mountains with its panoramic views, and everyone was mesmerized by what the chaplain said.

I originally had set up practice at the Academy as one of my little strategic ploys. Working out at the extra elevation would allow us to say, "Hey, no problem with the thin air here in Denver; it was 2,000 feet higher where we practiced." Thin air—even basketball, the NCAAs—was the farthest thing from our minds now.

We put a patch on our uniforms to remember Joe, but there was no dramatic dedication of the season to him or anything like that. This was family business, sad family business. I sent my Big East championship watch back to his home and he was buried with it, along with a UConn flag.

Sheila McGinn, on the phone, tried to tell me how much the team and I had meant to Joe, how much we had done for him. I told her it was the other way around, that his everyday courage meant more to me and to the team than he ever knew, that we gained so much more from knowing him than he ever gained from us.

And that was the truth.

.   .   .

The most notable fact about our tournament-opening 91–66 win over Texas–San Antonio, I suppose, was that the UConn coach did not appear for the confrontation. The coach was back in his hotel room, feeling quite ill.

I traced the virus back to my brother, Bill, now a cardiologist in Boston, who'd come to the Big East. After he left the tournament he became so sick he had to cancel his appointments for the first time in his medical career. He left the bug with me, so I had to cancel an appointment with the NCAAs for the first time.

I gave it the Gipper try—put on my suit and got ready to go—but I quickly found out that I couldn't be anywhere that was more than six steps from porcelain fixtures. I watched the game in the hotel with Pat. Well, Pat was in the room. I don't think there was much conversation. As much as I love her, she could have been Joey Whelton, coming down to the table to talk during that exhibition in London. When I watch this team play, I watch this team play.

Six or seven years ago, the tickets at Gampel for members of the players' families and for prospective recruits were shifted quietly from behind our bench to the other side of the arena. This protected the moms and dads and potential strong forwards from learning any new words or hearing any old words strung together in configurations that were a bit different from what they were used to. Poor Pat—she could only move to the other side of the room.

I railed at the usual things . . .

I wanted Rash to get back on defense . . .

I wanted us to show more enthusiasm, spirit . . .

I also was able to rail at commercials.

Do you realize how many commercials there are during these games? The worst part came 10 minutes from the end. CBS—the way it declares elections decided about two minutes after the polls have closed, with maybe 10 ballots counted—decided we had won the game easily. They switched to another game!

I wound up calling my son Jeff, who was at McNichols Arena. Jeff had to call back on the cell phone every few minutes with an update. Dave Leitao did a fine job replacing me on the bench, but that didn't mean I wasn't antsy the entire time.

I like to hold the clicker, remember. I like to be in charge.

*   *   *

E. J. Harrison scored 12 points for us in the game. It was nice to see. (Or hear for the last 10 minutes.) He is our walk-on who is not a walk-on. He is our basketball player without a scholarship. I guess that's how we refer to him, but he's also a very special kid.

The normal walk-ons (and we had two of them: Ed Tonella, of Tucson, Arizona, and Richard Moore, of Hamden, Connecticut) are kids who come out of an open tryout and basically are practice players. They are around to fill out the cast in practice, to step in when other players are hurt or tired. For their first year on the team, they dress in a separate room—where I made Antric dress at the start of the season—and they are sort of the common men, the gym rats, enjoying their time in the big leagues.

E.J. is another story. He was the leading scorer at Western Connecticut State University (Division III) for two years. He was a kid from Danbury we never had recruited, didn't know existed, until his coach called us after that second year. E.J. wanted to transfer. We looked at some tape, saw a truly fast 6'1" guard, saw he'd averaged 19 points a game, and brought him into the operation. He never was considered a walk-on and dressed in the big locker room from the beginning because he was a viable player. He easily could see some minutes that meant something in a game that meant something. He was that good.

Albert Mouring, however, was better. E.J. hadn't played much in either his junior or senior seasons because he was behind Albert, who was behind Khalid and Ricky. Albert, a 6'3" sophomore, could become a star with us in his last two years. He is a rare kind of shooter, instant points. He is the one guy on our bench who can come into a game and score in a hurry, the guy who simply deflates the other team.

Albert is probably the quietest kid I've ever coached, so quiet he and Joe Sharpe, who also is quiet, probably could drive to New York and back, never say a word to each other, and be perfectly happy. He is from Preston, Maryland, a tiny town. The University of Maryland was making a push for him, but pushed a little too hard trying to make him commit. Albert isn't the kind of kid who can be pushed. He wound up with us, thank you very much.

He needed a few more points on his SATs, so we put him on the Souleymane program for a semester—working at Schilberg Integrated Metals in Willimantic, studying at night. Albert did the whole thing— renting the apartment, working on the loading dock, growing up in a hurry. He made his score on the SATs and was able to join us for the second semester last year.

He sprained his knee in the last regular-season game this year against Syracuse and sat out the Big East and Texas–San Antonio games. That opened room for E.J., whose 25 minutes and 12 points were the highlight of his UConn career. Albert was back for the first test of the knee against New Mexico in our second game in Denver.

No problem with the knee; no problem with New Mexico. We scored the first 17 points of the first half. We scored the first 13 points of the second half. We won, 78–56. We were on to the Sweet Sixteen—again.

* * *

The university was in spring break, so it was easier for us simply to stay on the road and go directly to Phoenix, the next stop. This would mean we would be on the road for 12 straight days if we made it to the Elite Eight. Add in four days at the Big East and we would have been on the road for 16 out of 19 days. And if we got to the Final Four, it could be as much as 22 of 27 days.

An obvious question might be: Do these kids really go to school?

The term *student-athlete* had come under scrutiny during the weekend in our bracket of the tournament. A former employee at the University of Minnesota claimed to have written term papers for Minnesota basketball players. Four players, including two starters, were suspended. Minnesota was dumped, 75–63, in a small upset by 10th-seeded Gonzaga, which then pulled a much bigger upset, dropping our old friends from Stanford, the second seed in our region, 82–74.

Ted Taigen, our academic adviser, was bothered by the whole Minnesota affair.

"It made me sick to my stomach," he said. "It feeds the popular stereotype that athletes have everything handed to them. That isn't the case. Certainly not here. These kids are students. They're doing their work every day."

Take any 15 kids in the college environment and look at the range of academic abilities. There probably will be a few kids who really want to learn, a few who struggle, and a majority who are plugging ahead toward graduation. You'd find the same range on our basketball team. There are kids who want to goof off, kids who really care, kids who are on the dean's list.

Ted has been with us, full time during the season, for five years. He runs a study hall every night when we are home. He pretty much is the face of academia when we are on the road. He sets up a room at the hotel with four computers and a couple of printers, and kids can connect to the virtual classroom and get assignments, tests, quizzes, and notes from their classes. They can fax in term papers. They can E-mail questions. The computer has made the link to college so much easier than it was.

"It's hard, though, for some kinds of courses," Ted says. "It's almost impossible to take a language course during a basketball season. You miss so much by not speaking the language in class, by not going to the language labs. You fall behind so far on a trip like this, you can't catch up. Any kind of cumulative course, each step based on the last step, is very hard. Math is hard for players to take during the season.

"We usually tell kids to take languages or math in the fall. Or in summer school."

Ted is the guy we needed and wanted when I first arrived and Phil Gamble and Cliff Robinson flunked off the team. He monitors kids' work. He encourages them. He calls nightly. He revels in his job. He played a year of basketball at Colorado State and still plays basketball every noon with assorted chubby professors and grad students. I tell him that one of my first changes on campus—and this is true—was that I banned players from playing in noontime games with guys like him. Ted's expertise is not the pick and roll.

"There are moments of triumph that no one else notices," he says about his job. "We were going to an NCAA game last year, and Ricky and Rash were arguing in the back of the bus about something in *King Lear*. I remember I just sat back with a smile on my face."

While we were in Denver, a number of the kids were doing papers for a political science course they were taking. The topic was something like "Relate the character of Machiavelli to modern-day life."

Ted says three or four papers had to be marked "confidential" when they were faxed back to campus. I wonder who the kids decided was a Machiavellian character in their daily lives?

.   .   .

The Sweet Sixteen put us into the middle of a great little soap opera at the America West Arena. Dr. Tom Davis, the 60-year-old Iowa coach, already had been fired. He had been told before the season started that his contract would not be renewed and he had the option to resign. He decided to stay. His players were playing their brains out for him, making a tournament run to make the university's administration look bad. There was enough emotion at work here to win at least a couple of daytime Emmys.

I'm not sure what our role was. Maybe we were the network executives who had arrived to pull the plug on the whole show.

I was more than familiar with Dr. Tom. He was at BC for a stretch while I was at Northeastern 20 years ago. He was younger and thinner at the time, and certainly didn't have the white hair he had now. I—my funny mirror talking here—looked exactly the way I do today.

Dr. Tom was a basketball inventor, an innovator. His teams always were interesting to watch, hard to play against. He was the first guy I ever heard talk about the positions in the lineup as "the one, the two," et cetera. Everybody uses those terms now. He was a believer in the bounce pass, the fast break, the full-court press. Another thing he might have started: He always made a substitution after his team made a free throw to gain a stop in action to set up the press.

My Northeastern teams had played his BC teams four times and lost all four games. He had gone from BC to Stanford, then to Iowa, where he had been the coach for 13 years. He was conducting himself with dignity and style in his present lame-duck situation.

"It's not something I've used as a coaching tool," he said. "It's something I've just lived with. I haven't ducked any questions. I haven't told any untruths. The tournament and trying to move forward override all other issues, as they should."

His present team was interesting, as usual. It had a lot of size, a lot of bulk, and wasn't very fast—sort of a team made up of football players in their off-season, but still followed the Dr. Tom philosophies of pressing and running. It would be the first team to try to press us all year. It also would try to run over us rather than past us.

This became the most physical game I've ever coached.

The pushing, shoving, bumping, and talking began early and never really stopped. The officials did not seem to mind this kind of game, Iowa didn't seem to mind, and our kids didn't seem to mind. I was the one who minded.

When the first half ended, UConn ahead by five, there was a situation at halfcourt. An Iowa kid, Joey Range, heading toward the locker room, threw a little elbow at Khalid. Khalid, heading in the other direction, turned and came back at Range and pushed him. Everyone else also turned, and the two teams began to get together. I think Joe Sharpe, who grabbed Khalid, and Beau Archibald, one of our redshirts, who pinned Edmund (Edmund!) in a hurry, probably should have been our Chevrolet Players of the Game. The officials reviewed the incident on a TV monitor and decided everyone could stay for the second half.

I jumped on the kids in the locker room. I told them we were concentrating on winning the fights instead of the game. I said we had no composure. I said the next kid I saw yapping at someone else, looking for trouble, would yap and look from a seat next to me on the bench.

Iowa, to give Dr. Tom credit, stayed close. The game was tied, 53–53, with 10:10 left before we went on a 14–4 run to pull away. Oh, and here was another thing Dr. Tom might have had in his coaching bag before anyone else: fouls at the end to lengthen the game. We scored our last 14 points from the line for a 78–68 win to pull the plug on the drama.

I watched the other semifinal to take some notes on Florida, our next opponent in the Elite Eight on Saturday. I had some very good notes, too, on Florida.

And then Gonzaga won the game in overtime.

● ● ●

Gonzaga was the absolute last team The Coach Who Never Had Been To The Final Four wanted to see standing in the way. The psychology of this game was all wrong. The kids had been building to this moment from that afternoon with the sad faces a year ago in Greensboro. They had worked through the brackets as soon as the brackets were announced, figuring which heavyweight would be the final obstacle to the Final Four trip. Stanford was an obvious possibility. No. 3 seed, North Carolina, would be fine poetic justice. Gonzaga?

No one had thought about Gonzaga.

"Coach," Tom Moore said, almost reluctantly, after watching his tapes, "this team is good."

He hadn't given this report for Texas–San Antonio, New Mexico, or Iowa. He did for Gonzaga.

The small Jesuit college from Spokane, Washington, named after St. Aloysius Gonzaga, a 16th-century Jesuit who died of the plague, had sent out this year's giant-killer to the tournament. The Zags were making school history with just about every three-pointer. They were loose and confident and had that Blues Brothers look, like they were on a mission from God.

The casual fan, sitting at home, had adopted them. I would have adopted them, too, if I were the casual fan. They were a carload of Don Quixotes. If they ever reached the Final Four, it would be a story for the NCAA ages. I can't think of a team in recent history—maybe Cedric Maxwell's UNC–Charlotte team in 1977 was close—that had come from as far back in the public consciousness to get to the Final Four. Cedric's team at least had one certified pro prospect, Cedric. These guys, on paper, had none.

What did they have? They had some nice size. They had some good ball handlers. They had some devastating three-point shooters, averaging 50.8 percent in the tournament. That was the formula for an upset that had worked against Minnesota, Stanford, and Florida. It scared me to death.

"Ricky Moore spoke at my daughter's elementary school this year," Ted Taigen said. "A kid asked him about last year in Greensboro. I couldn't believe Ricky's answer. He talked long and eloquently about how he had lost that game for the team. He, himself, personally. I choke up when I describe it. He took the whole burden on himself. I couldn't believe how it had stuck with him so, how he was carrying around this weight all the time. It was amazing to me."

That was the exact weight he was supposed to carry. That was the weight all the kids were supposed to carry. I had given them the weight in Greensboro and reminded them of it again and again. It had been important and helpful for the entire season. It was supposed to be important when we hit this same situation, this Armageddon, this apocalypse.

Armageddon had turned into a three-foot putt.

Ever try to make a three-foot putt for money?

*　　*　　*

Everybody was wound up. The assistant coaches said they couldn't remember when the team had been so tight. Everybody was tight. This was a shaky game, start to finish. It was one of those games where if we were down six, we were in big trouble. If they were down six, they had us right where they wanted us. There was no way to feel easy.

Ricky did the big defensive job, shutting down guard Matt Santangelo, the protégé of Gonzaga grad John Stockton, holding him to 1 for 9 from the outside. Rip did the big offensive job, 9 for 16 from the floor, 21 points. Kevin had a giant game on the boards, 10 offensive rebounds, 15 total, 13 points. Khalid, alas, was among the missing for most of the day. He had two quick fouls, had to sit for 15 minutes in the first half, then was 0 for 12 from the floor and the man he was guarding, little Quentin Hall, was 6 for 12, with 18 points.

Gonzaga never would go away.

The Zags threw every defense imaginable at us, harried us to 36.9 percent shooting, no three-pointers, none. While we paid attention to the perimeter, their big men proved to be better than expected. Their poise never wavered. The Zags were a piece of lint on a Sunday suit, impossible to flick off.

"When you sit on the sidelines, you get a feel for who wants to play, who doesn't want to play," Dave said. "I'll tell you what: They run great offense, they body you inside, they play great defense. Their big guys are as skilled as any we've seen this year. They've got pieces they can use to play big-time basketball."

Our rebounding kept us alive. Our defense kept us alive.

"If your A game isn't there, you always can win with your A effort," Rip said. "Everybody played with a lot of intensity, really picked it up on defense. When we needed a stop, we did that. That's the type of team we are."

The lint was still there with 35.9 seconds left on the clock. Hall hit an off-balance, how-did-he-do-that three-pointer to bring the Zags to within a point, 63–62. I remember thinking, *Oh, no. This could be a sign of bad things to come,* but I told the team, "We're all right. We're okay. Let's just keep the game in our hands."

And then we won it, 67–62, on free throws.

Khalid hit two. Kevin hit two.

And we were in the Final Four.

.　　.　　.

Tim Tolokan always used to complain that he had no pictures of me to put on press guides and programs. His photographers never, not once, had caught a picture of me smiling on the sideline. This probably was because I never smile much on the sideline. Tim Tolokan now says he has enough pictures of me smiling to carry him for the next decade. They all came from the next few minutes.

Rash poured the water down my back.

Khalid hugged me.

"Coach," he said, "I want you to go into the Hall of Fame the right way. Without any questions."

I began to celebrate as if it were the end of the final day of third grade before summer vacation. I smiled. I cried. I stood in the middle of the floor and hugged Pat.

We all have moments of overpowering grief in our life. There are so few moments of overpowering joy. This was one of them.

It wasn't so much a feeling of "Yeah, I finally got there"—no, that wasn't it at all. I still had that feeling that I wasn't one bit better as a coach or a person for making the Final Four. It was the sight of all these people who were so happy, happy for me, people who said, "Yeah, you finally got there." I was the target. That was what got to me. My happiness was a reflection of their happiness. I saw such happiness in their faces—for me.

The players . . . I push them and prod them, beg them and scream at them. There are times, driving home in your car, sitting up in bed late at night, you question yourself: *Have I gone too far? Am I too tough? Do they understand what I'm doing? Do I have the right to put the burden on them? I put it on myself every day, but that's one thing. Do I have the right to put it on them?*

Travis Knight. I killed him every day for four years when he was here. I was all over him, pushing and pushing and pushing. And then it was done. He was drafted by the Chicago Bulls in the first round, but they didn't really want him because they had Jordan and Pippen and were champions already. They wanted him to go to Europe. I stepped in, got involved, and told them this was unacceptable. They wound up trading him to Los Angeles, and now he has the $26 million contract.

I remember him saying to me, in the middle of the thing with the Bulls, "Hey, you really like me, don't you?" It was a revelation. *Well, yeah, of course I really like you.* That's what it's all about. I like 'em all. (Okay, some

I like better than others.) That's why I do this. *I do this because I like you, I want you to be better, the best you can be.*

To see the look on these kids' faces, to see they understood that it all was worth it—I was taken back by that as much as anything.

The place where I lost it was the locker room. I tried to give a speech, and as I looked around I saw Mass cards for Joe McGinn that were in some of the kids' lockers. Mass cards and little stuffed Husky dogs. I broke down. I couldn't talk.

"That's okay, Coach," different players said.

"We understand."

"We do."

There was so much involved: the death of Joe, the birth of my grand-daughter, everything wrapped up together. I started thinking about Cliff Robinson deciding to stay with us after he had been ruled ineligible. I thought about Ray Allen and Doron, who had really wanted to go to the Final Four. They were part of this. Everybody was.

There always had been speculation about what I would be like if I ever did get past this door. Would I tell a hundred people to stuff it? Would I stand on my little stage and say, "Well, how about those apples, you idiots?" There was none of that. That wasn't in the equation. Not one bit. There was only this overwhelming joy.

I even could see the joy in the faces of the Horde. Eleven papers in Connecticut cover our team. Fifteen writers minimum, sometimes more, cover every one of our games on the road. They've written some tough, tough things about me, some of these guys. To see them come up . . . "Congratulations, Coach." They felt good for me. I could see it. It wasn't fake.

I thought about all the coaches out there, guys who work so hard, do a good job, and never get here. I wasn't Bobby Knight or Mike Krzyzewski. I was one of those guys. I represented them. I remember watching Lute Olsen when he finally won with Arizona. I don't really know Lute Olsen, wouldn't say we were friends or anything, but I was really rooting for him. He was one of us. He was another guy. I was glad for him when he won.

It was the same way people were glad for me.

I could feel it.

That was why I smiled. That was why I cried.

*   *   *

A reporter from the *Los Angeles Times*, Bill Plaschke, caught me as the celebrations were winding down. He got me talking about Joe McGinn. He sort of conned me into it. I started crying again. He wrote a beautiful story. One of the anecdotes was a story about the time a substitute teacher took over Joe's grammar school class for a week. Joe changed his name for the week to Michael Jordan. He handed in every assignment using the name Michael Jordan instead of Joe McGinn. The teacher found out; Joe wound up in the principal's office.

Think about it.

Rip had his old picture of Michael Jordan in his locker for luck. The other kids had this new picture of this other Michael Jordan in their lockers.

How could we lose?

Chapter 9

THE FINAL FOUR

Jim:

Nice going. I don't see how it happened since the Duke coach got a number of awards for being the smartest coach going and he had the two best players, according to the experts. You know, you made a lot of people mad. Billy Packer may kill himself. Of course, Dick Vitale will just switch sides. . . .

I broke a tooth, so I took a couple of pain pills. At the half, I made some cheese toast and sat down. That's the last thing I remember. I woke up with a piece of toast on my chest and some guy talking about UConn winning the game. I never saw a play in the second half. It was seeing the K[rzyzewski] family crying instead of the Calhoun family that told me The Calhoun Boys had struck again. . . .

Abe Lemons
Houston, TX

I used to run marathons before my knee cartilage turned to old leather. I ran Boston three times and New York three times. I had some tests done when I was in my early thirties and found out that by nature I have the cholesterol of a jelly doughnut or hot-fudge sundae. I started running to lower my cholesterol and, my nature being what it is, pretty soon I was wondering what it would take to beat that Frank Shorter guy.

I used to run all the time while I was at Northeastern. A dean at the school, Dr. Tom Kerr, a good guy, a friend, would run with me. He was descended from Northern Irish Protestant forefathers and had an orange shamrock tattooed on one ankle. I'd tell him to pull up his sock before we both got killed as we ran the Boston streets.

The thing about running marathons—outside of the fact they made you skinny and feel awful good and awful bad at the same time—was that you missed the party. You maybe *were* the party, the reason friends and relatives had gathered along the course, but you never could enjoy it. The night before the race, you couldn't join the fun because you were in training for the big day. The night after the race, you couldn't join the party because you just couldn't walk very well, much less go out dancing.

The Final Four—if you're coaching or playing for one of the teams—is pretty much the same thing. You're the reason everyone you know from your past, present, or even future has gathered. You can't spend much time with any of them.

Half the state of Connecticut seemed to have plopped itself down in the Tampa–St. Pete area. VISA cards everywhere had to be screaming, pressed to their limits. The families and the extended families and the extended families of the extended families of the players had arrived. The whole thing seemed to be a Fourth of July picnic with basketball instead of fireworks.

"Jake's godfather coached him in biddy basketball, third grade," Joe Voskuhl said. "This actually happened: He brought the team around him one day and said 'Look, I don't have any children. You're my children and I'm glad to coach you. I only want one thing from each of you. I want a promise. If any of you ever makes it to the Final Four, I want two tickets.' Well, not only is he here, we're staying at his house."

That kid, Clint Ray, the one who had the miracle when Jake went back to Houston? He was here. Walking fine. Pam Long, Rip's mom, was here. Her youngest son, Chauncey, age six, had the flu a year ago when we were in the Sweet Sixteen. Pam stayed home with him instead of going to the game. That was the game where Rip hit the shot as the buzzer sounded to beat Washington. Pam jumped around her apartment cheering and at the same time vowing she would never miss a big game again. Chauncey was here, too. He also didn't want to miss the big game.

Khalid's entire family was here, finding a mosque to celebrate Eid ul-Adha, the Day of Sacrifice, an Islamic holy day. Souleymane, our other Muslim, his family wasn't here. He had tried for a month to get a visa for his brother to come from Senegal, but had run into a U.S. Immigration roadblock. At least the game was being broadcast back to Dakar—it would be the first time his family ever had seen him play. Souleymane was adopted for the time being by E. J. Harrison's family, which also was here. Everybody had somebody.

Ray Allen was here. He couldn't find a commercial flight that could get him here on time from his day job with the Milwaukee Bucks, so he'd chartered a plane for $20,000. Ah, the NBA. A bunch of former players was here. Howie Dickenman, my longtime assistant, was here. His Central Connecticut team, in fact, had fallen only one playoff game short of making the NCAA dance itself.

I had 96 tickets for each of the games. Pat handled all distribution. My brother and all my sisters except for Rose were here; Rose, with no planning or confidence, whichever it was, had booked a cruise for this week. Pat's large family was here. All their kids, our nieces and nephews, were here. My kids were here. Emily, my granddaughter, was here! The first time I ever saw her was when we checked into the Hyatt. She was waiting with her mom and dad in the lobby. She was a minor media star already.

"I'm the pessimist, Jennifer is the optimist," Jim junior said. "I never thought you could bring a four-week-old baby from Oregon to something like this. Jennifer said we should at least check with the doctor. I was the one who had to say to this pediatrician, 'Look, I know this sounds stupid, but have you ever heard of the Final Four? My dad is the coach of this basketball team, Connecticut. . . .' The doctor looked up and said, 'I graduated from Duke. Of course you have to be there.'"

Mother Shaun Vergauwen of the Franciscan Life Order was here. One year late. (Pat had brought along the key to the city to the Final Four. Thank you, Bowie.)

Bob Samuelson, my college roommate and good friend, was here. He had undergone a quadruple bypass on February 18. He still felt weak from the surgery. He'd said he shouldn't come. I'd countered with a dozen medical reasons why he should. Talking with my brother, Bill, the cardiologist, over the years, I have learned something about the workings of the human heart.

"What are you, a doctor?" Bob had said. "Where do you get this stuff?" He was here. He admitted that he felt better in the sun.

Joe McGinn's parents, Sheila and Joe, were here. They had to be.

"I can't go," Sheila had told me. "Really."

"Well, here's the thing," I'd said. "I'm buying the plane tickets and I'm buying the tickets to the game. If you're not using them, I'm tearing them up. Do you understand? Your son would want you to be here. Don't you think?"

They were here.

There were so many people I liked, loved, wanted to spend days with, weeks. I could hardly see any of them. I had decided early that this was the only course I could follow. This was a business trip. I had to cut out most of the nuances, the fun, concentrate on the matter at hand.

The only old friend I could give much attention was Jimmy O'Brien. He was the coach of Ohio State. And we weren't friends so much anymore.

*   *   *

That day on the beach in Puerto Rico in 1986 seemed as if it had happened a long, long time ago. I look back at it now, both of us just named as coaches in the Big East, Jimmy at BC and myself at UConn, and there is an innocence to the scene. We're both rookies in this famous league, no-names matched against these famous coaching legends who are staying in the same hotel. We both have these hopes, these plans, but no idea if they ever can be fulfilled. We're sitting with our wives, Jimmy and Chris, Pat and me, and we're all in this new and interesting position.

I never understood how the ice developed.

I liked Jimmy. I had known him for a long time. He was five or six years younger than I was, a terrific point guard at BC as a player for Bob Cousy. He went into coaching as an assistant under Dom Perno at UConn, and I'd see him at the conventions, out on the recruiting trail, around and about. I don't say we were best friends or anything, but we always enjoyed each other's company. We were family guys. Neither of us was a big drinker. He took the head job at St. Bonaventure, my Northeastern teams with Reggie played against him, and we had a couple of beers after the game. That kind of stuff.

The wars in the Big East sort of pulled us apart.

I guess it was our second year in the league. Or maybe the third. My team beat his team in a blowout, and after the game he walked right past me. He barely shook my hand.

"What the hell was that all about?" I remember saying. It all went from there.

We usually played BC twice a year and beat BC twice a year. If it was three times in a given year, we beat BC three times in a given year. A streak began that still hasn't stopped. My team beat Jimmy O'Brien's team 18 straight times. If BC had a bad team, we won. If BC had a good team, which it did sometimes, we had a better team. The streak seemed to have a momentum all of its own. A chilly momentum.

In the middle of it, a terrible thing happened. Jimmy's wife, Chris, 41 years old, died of a heart attack. He was left with two daughters, and he was spinning, knocked out by the whole thing. Pat and I went to the wake, and Dennis Wolff, the coach at BU, a former UConn player, took me aside and said, "Hey, you guys have to talk sometime." I wrote Jimmy a letter, telling him how sorry I was about Chris. We eventually did talk. Nothing big. There still was that distance.

In the spring of 1997 he left BC after an argument with the admissions office. His name came up for some jobs, and I was a person people would call. Because of the streak. How had I beaten this guy 18 times in a row? What was wrong? I told the people that nothing was wrong. We usually were better. End of story.

I thought Jimmy had evolved into a terrific offensive coach through the years. His point guard mentality showed through into his coaching. If he had a kid who could hit a 14-foot jump shot, then there were going to be 86 ways the kid would be freed to hit that 14-foot jump shot. I told this to the people who asked.

When he got the Ohio State job that spring, he called me. He thanked me for the things I'd said. I said I'd meant them.

Ohio State turned out to be magic for him. In two years he'd pulled off one of the most spectacular turnarounds in NCAA history. He'd taken a team that finished last in the Big Ten in his first year to a team that finished first in the Big Ten this year. He'd beaten St. John's and Mike Jarvis, 77–74, in the South Regional to reach the Final Four. (Jarvis, Dr. Tom, now Jimmy . . . it all was a bit weird, these people from my personal history. I kept waiting for Ralph Edwards to say, "Jim Calhoun, this is your life.") Now Jimmy and I were matched in the semis of the Final Four.

On Thursday night there was a big banquet, the NCAA Coaches Salute Dinner in St. Petersburg. We sat at the same head table. A nice thaw began.

Jimmy, when he took the microphone, did a routine describing my arrival at the event. He said I shook the hand of Tom Izzo of Michigan State and congratulated Izzo and told him, "It's great to see you here." Jimmy said I did the same thing with Mike Krzyzewski of Duke: "Great season, great that you're back, great to see you." Jimmy described my greeting to Jimmy, the streak in mind, as 10 times more effusive.

"And Jimmy," I supposedly said. "It's *really great* to see you here."

Everybody knew the situation. Everybody laughed.

Dave Solomon from the *New Haven Register* sat down with Jimmy that day and did a column. Someone gave it to me. In it Jimmy described the day on the beach, and then explained a lot of things.

Jimmy described his side in the fracture in our relationship. He said it was an issue of maturity, that he never could separate the competitiveness on the court from life off the court. He said he hadn't been able to handle the losing. The streak.

It made me think a lot about myself and my job. I'm as competitive as any person you'll ever meet. I've said that. For those two hours during that game, the only people who matter to me are the five people on the floor in blue or white shirts and the seven or eight people in blue or white shirts on the bench. I don't care about the opposing coach, the referees, the score-keeper, anybody. Just those players and what they do. I can see how someone else could look at me and feel he was at a disadvantage, that I'm pushing, pushing, getting away with too much.

Coaching basketball is a tough profession for friendships, because the results all count. The *W* stays forever next to your name. The *L* stays forever. I say that to the Horde all the time: "You guys get an *L*, write a bad column, and a day later it goes out with the trash. My bad column goes into the record book."

In coaching a game, you have two guys fighting for the same thing, fighting for their livelihoods, really, because if I have too many *L*'s and you have too many *W*'s, I could be gone. A bunch of coaches have drifted apart. That's what happened with Jimmy and me.

I talked to him about Dave Solomon's column the next day and he repeated to me all the things he'd said to Solomon. I think we're better now. We made plans to get together soon, and I really hope we do.

Maybe we're both more mature.

Maybe the fact we're 500 miles away from each other now—and in different conferences—means something, too.

.   .   .

The guy who had done the most to turn around Ohio State's fortunes, along with Jimmy, was point guard Scoonie Penn. He was the little thermonuclear device Jimmy had in his pocket when he showed up in Columbus, a junior transfer from BC whom we knew only too well. He'd been a legitimate star in the Big East as both a freshman and a sophomore. He had to sit out that first year in Ohio State, then was the catalyst in the worst-to-first rise.

He was a Massachusetts kid and yes, we had a good chance to recruit him. And yes, we had looked at him in high school. And yes, we had decided he was too small to play in our league. And yes, we were mistaken. There are some decisions you'd take back in a moment. Scoonie could score points in a hurry, and he was like Khalid, getting his whole team moving.

That meant we put Ricky on him.

It is a luxury having a great defensive player. You can simply put him on the floor and remove a major weapon from the other team's offense. Ricky has such great feet, is so athletic, he's almost in front of his man even before his man starts to move. He's like the great football cornerback, arriving at the ball before the wide receiver.

This was what he did with Scoonie. He harassed him, thwarted him, put him one step off his rhythm, holding him to only 11 points on 3-of-13 shooting as we put together a workmanlike 64–58 win. It was defensive dominance, an aspect of the game that never gets the proper attention. Ricky brings it to every game we play.

Rip was on fire on offense, 10 for 17, 24 points. Khalid was back from his 0-for-12 at Gonzaga, going 8 for 15, with 18 points. Ohio State tried to overplay on defense, and Rip and Khalid rolled past to the hoop. We tore open the zone Ohio State tried. We just went hard to the basket every time in this one. *Spurtability* was Khalid's word of the month, and we definitely had spurtability. This was one of those games where I felt from the beginning that we would win, and even when Ohio State closed at the end of the first half, I thought we were in control. We always were on the verge of another spurt.

The defense would carry us if that spurt never came.

"I've seen Mateen Cleaves, I've seen some of the great players in the Big East, like Jason Hart of Syracuse . . . it seems they all have bad shooting games against us," I told the Horde at the press conference. "Continually, if you asked me for the MVP of our games, Ricky Moore would be there. He cut the head off the dragon tonight for us. Scoonie, to me, is how it all happens for Ohio State. As Scoonie goes, so goes Ohio State."

Scoonie was going home.

Our kids were happy—it was a great win, in the semifinals of the national championship—but you know what? They weren't much different from how they would be after a big win at Syracuse in the Carrier Dome on a Monday night. There was mixture of joy and unfinished business that I liked.

"I remember the Seton Hall game with Michigan [1989] when Rumeal Robinson, who was from Boston, hit those two free throws to win," Kevin told reporters about his first NCAA memory. "I watched it with my dad.

"Ever since then, the dream has been there for me. I watched Chris Webber play for a national championship and Grant Hill play for a championship, and that's where I wanted to be. It's kind of like living in a fantasy."

One more game. Duke.

●   ●   ●

The first time a UConn basketball team played against Duke was in 1964 in the Eastern Regional finals. I was a student at AIC. A young former Duke assistant, Fred Shabel, had taken the head job at UConn and worked a small miracle. His first team had captured the Yankee Conference and the automatic berth in the 32-team NCAA field. It had upset Temple and then Princeton, Dom Perno putting a defensive blanket on All-American and future senator and presidential candidate Bill Bradley. There was euphoria in Storrs, the Huskies one game away from the Final Four.

Duke was next.

Duke beat UConn, 101–54.

No big moment probably ever was turned more convincingly into a bad moment. The Blue Devils had Jack Marin and Jeff Mullins, a pair of All-Americans and future pros, and they embarrassed the Huskies. UConn guards couldn't get the ball past midcourt. UConn star center Toby Kimball was sandwiched by Duke giants under the basket. The score at the end of the first half was Duke 62, UConn 27. Duke shot 67 percent from the floor in the half.

I guess if you wanted to show how far UConn basketball had to travel, this game was it. A 47-point loss to Duke in the Elite Eight was the high point for the program for the next 26 years. "Remember that great team in '64?" "Yeah, got smoked by Duke in the end."

When we made our Dream Season run in 1990, with Nadav and Chris Smith and everybody, sure enough, there was Duke, waiting at the same time, same station. There was Christian Laettner, hitting that accursed shot. ("At least he had the right first name," a minister said in church in Storrs the next day.) Next year in the Sweet Sixteen? Duke 81, Connecticut 67.

There wasn't a long rivalry between the two schools—we also split two regular-season games—but what did exist was lopsided and one-dimensional. The UConn fan thought of Duke the way the Red Sox fan thinks of the New York Yankees. The Duke fan thought of UConn . . . well, the Duke fan probably didn't think of UConn at all.

In the nineties, Duke has been the preeminent college basketball force. As good as we have been, Duke has been a light in the window at the far end of the road. Under Mike Krzyzewski, the Blue Devils have won two national championships, reached the Final Four five times. What Duke has wanted basically is what Duke has gotten. We have brought some very good players—some great players—to Storrs, but not one of them was stolen from Duke in a direct recruiting battle. Duke has been the college basketball colossus.

Even during the 1998–99 season, even when we were 19–0, the specter of Duke always hovered over us. Take away that last-second loss to Cincinnati at the beginning of the year and Duke certainly would have been No. 1, wire to wire. Duke was the team with the pedigree, with the seven McDonald's All-Americans. Duke was the team with the history. We were the newcomers to the table. The sportswriters were calling this tournament the "Duke Invitational." Duke led the nation in scoring, with an average of 92.3 points, and in margin of victory, 25.4 points. Duke led the nation, period. The big debate was not about whether this team would win the national championship, but where it would be ranked in the list of all-time college basketball units. There was considerable support for the idea that this was the best college team ever, the best team ever to play the game.

My biggest fear was that image. I didn't want us to get down early, to suddenly decide we were playing against DUKE. I wanted us to attack, attack, attack. Challenge. I didn't think a lot of teams had done that against Duke this year. Half its games—more than half—had been won during warm-ups, when the other team read the name on the front of that blue shirt.

I did think, with all its young players, though, Duke was a little bit overrated. . . .

I certainly thought, 9½ point underdogs, we were underrated. . . .

Then again, maybe Fred Shabel thought that, too, in 1964. It was time to find out.

*　　*　　*

The chance that a great basketball game will evolve is largely determined by the two teams involved. It is tough to dance if one partner doesn't want to dance. You know that thing you told girls, "I can't fast-dance because my knee is hurt, but I'll slow-dance"? If one team is working that philosophy, there isn't much you can do. If you're playing Princeton or Temple, well, you're pretty much going to play at their slow-dance pace.

Two teams wanted to fast-dance here. I never had second thoughts about that. Duke wanted to push the ball up the floor. Mike's offense is very basic, easy to scout, very difficult to defend. We weren't much different. Neither team, really, would have any gimmicks, any surprises. We both prefered the jitterbug to the waltz.

I'd been to the Duke campus in Durham, North Carolina, about four weeks earlier to film a Nike commercial with Mike, Tubby Smith of Kentucky, and Lute Olsen of Arizona. While we were sitting around, just talking, I asked Mike how his teams had pounded Maryland twice during the year. I thought Maryland was a very good team.

"Maryland presses us every time down the court," Mike said. "That's the way [coach] Gary Williams likes to play. He winds up giving us the open floor. We have good ball handlers, and once we get past that press we have 4 on 3, 3 on 2, and we take advantage of the situation. We're a lot like you. You'd do very well against Maryland. You play the same way we do."

I wasn't really looking for information, just talking, but this confirmed what I thought about the press. We would press Duke, but only in the 2-2-1, always with two men back at the basket. I didn't want many of those situations where Duke had the extra man.

I never especially worried about our offense. Duke, simply by the way it played, would give us chances to score. I was more worried about stopping Duke from scoring than about our scoring. One thing we had picked up from film was that Duke always switched on the pick-and-roll. It was pretty much a team rule, something most teams don't do. We wanted to run the pick-and-roll with big men and little men to create mismatches. If Elton Brand were forced to guard Rip or Khalid, 22 feet from the basket, Rip or Khalid had an enormous advantage on the outside. They could get free for their shot in a moment. We wanted that.

The keys were the same as I had outlined during the pregame talks:

1. Double Elton with two big men every time he touches the ball.
2. Get the ball out of William Avery's hands.
3. Don't get in a total shootout.

Ricky, after much discussion, would guard Avery at the start. Khalid would guard Trajan Langdon, conscious all the time of the three-point shot. Rip would guard Chris Carrawell, playing off him to turn him into a jump shooter rather than a slasher to the basket. Kevin would guard Shane Battier but always be ready to step over to help out Jake with Elton.

We kicked around these matchups so much that even now I have trouble remembering them, some kind of Freudian thing, because they never were settled in my head. Ricky would wind up playing a lot against Langdon as the game evolved, maybe 60 percent of the time. I guess we wished we had about three Rickys. That was our problem on defense. We wished we could be sure of shutting down everyone everywhere.

The first half was pretty much what I expected. Terrific basketball. Were we intimidated by the word on the front of the Duke shirts? No. Not at all. Battier would say later that this was the first team he'd seen all year that looked like it *wanted* to play Duke. Did we fall behind quickly? Yes, but the score was 9–2 and Duke had made some tough baskets and we had missed some easy ones. Was the pick-and-roll, the big-and-little mismatch, available? Very much so. Khalid used it. Rip used it. Was the big-man double on Elton working? Yes. The press on Avery, forcing him to give up the ball? Also working. Ricky, in fact, was a terror on both ends of the floor.

One of the side stories of the week had been the remembered fact that Ricky and William Avery had been friends and teammates at Westside High in Augusta. They were two kids from Hazel Street, Ricky from the 2600 block, William from 2700. Ricky was two years older, but they would meet on the street and go down to Big Oak, the local park, where the rims were two feet higher than normal to keep players from dunking. They played together one year at Westside, winning the state title as Ricky averaged 21 points and William 19.

This was Big Oak brought to the big time. Ricky not only was his normal defensive self, he was leading our challenge on offense. He was as free and easy as if this were the playground and the Reynolds brothers, the scourges of the Big Oak court, were waiting for the next game.

"You can't guard me," I heard Ricky say.

He had scored 13 points by the half.

We trailed, 39–37.

It was the 10th time we had trailed an opponent at the half this year. I liked the way we were playing.

. . .

"Keep doing what we're doing" was my message in the locker room. No dramatics. "Remember to be tight on offense. You got a little loose here and there, heading toward the shootout. Also stay tight on defense. Twenty minutes to go. A chance for history. Our time."

I felt we needed someone to step forward and do more scoring for us because I knew Ricky wouldn't score another 13 points in the second half, just wouldn't. (He scored none, as it turned out, concentrating on defense.) I felt we had to be judicious with the use of the press, putting it on at strategic moments. I also thought we had to keep our attention on Mr. Brand—no nonsense there. I felt pretty good, really.

I even thought the referees were doing a great job. (Okay, I'll pause while you pick yourself off the floor.) No, they were. They were into the fast dance, the flow of the game, as much as the players were. Maybe they were letting some hand checking go, the Duke guards against our guards, but maybe they also were letting some whacks against Elton go in our double teams. The ref we knew best in the threesome, Timmy Higgins from our conference, always has been a terrific referee.

Jake, I know, had been quoted as saying he hoped Higgins would work the game. Jake is a tough player to officiate. He is arms and legs, and he forces you to make a lot of decisions. Some referees, calling a tight game, send him to the bench early every night. Timmy lets him play a little.

No one would foul out in the entire game. Fouls were never a problem for either team. No one would complain about the officials. That's a good game right there.

∘　∘　∘

The second half was more of the same. Back and forth. There would be 14 ties and eight changes of the lead before we were done. I liked the pace. Again, I always had the feeling we were ahead, even when the scoreboard didn't agree. They never could pull away from us for any length of time, and we always seemed on the verge of pulling away from them before they made some great play to stay in sight.

I wasn't afraid of a nail-biter at the end. We'd been a spotlight team all year, playing at our best not only in the biggest games, but in the biggest moments of the biggest games. That was a comfort in the back of my mind that mostly came from Khalid. If the game was close, there always was the feeling that Khalid would make good things happen at the end.

I liked the way our bench played. Souleymane played some good minutes against Elton. He slapped the ball out of Elton's hands once and picked it up and put it in the basket. All of Senegal cheered. Albert played some good minutes in place of Khalid, six points and good defense on William. All of Schilberg Metals in Willimantic cheered. Edmund gave us more minutes against Elton, always active. Edmund had been in an argument with Soule in our first practice in Tampa, the rage seeping out unexpectedly, but he was all right now; he was the 90 percent Edmund. Fine. Antric even gave us a minute of rest for the big men. Antric. He didn't forget his passport when he went to the scorer's table.

There was 3:50 left when Rip, who pretty much was doing what he wanted against Carrawell on offense, hit two foul shots to give us the lead, 70–68. Then there was a TV time-out. I thought it was time for us to make a statement. Elton was starting to get rolling in the last moments of the game, and our double team was not as effective. The Duke kids were looking more self-assured. We hadn't used the press in a while, but now I called for it again. I wanted us not only to press, but to press hard.

I think Duke was surprised by that. The press is a little more danger-
ous at this time of the game because of the chance that you could give
away something instead of making Duke earn it. No matter. We pressed
hard, and Ricky came around and just flicked the ball away from Avery.
Rip was open in the corner. He buried a three-pointer, as pretty a jump
shot as you'd ever want to see, the thigh and the foot and all problems of
the long season forgotten. This was how good he was supposed to be at the
start of the year—the best player in college basketball. We now were up by
five with 3:29 left. In essence, that was the game.

Or should have been.

Duke came back at us. Carrawell made one of two foul shots and then
the Blue Devils got the ball back again, down four. We played defense as if
we had invented it. No shots were open. None. As time ran out on the shot
clock, Battier tried an off-balance jumper. Ricky, guarding Trajan, dropped
off to chase the rebound. The rebound, weird, bounced off two or three
hands and came back directly to Trajan. He buried a three-pointer.

It was one of those shots that make you question if fate is against you.
We had done everything right, worked so hard. He made a terrific shot—
he made terrific shots thoughout the game—but he never should have had
it. Duke again trailed by one with 1:43 left.

In the next minute, Khalid hit a 10-foot runner for us off the pick-
and-roll, the big-little mismatch we'd exploited all night. William Avery hit
two foul shots. We ran some time off the clock and called time-out.

Thirty-four seconds left. A one-point game. We went right back to the
big-man-small-man matchup when we returned to the floor. It worked.
Khalid shook free, started to go up for the shot . . . and slipped. Carrawell
rebounded the miss.

Twenty-four seconds. A one-point game. Duke didn't call time-out.
That's a big question now—should Mike have called time-out?—but I
wouldn't have called time-out either. His team's strength was in the open
court. That was our team's strength, too.

Ricky, playing Trajan, heard Mike yell, "Take him, Trajan." This started
the sequence that won the ball game. There was a one-on-one battle

between our best defender and their best shooter. Ricky, the way he'd done it for the entire year, for his entire underpublicized career, anticipated Trajan's spin move and stepped in front of him. Trajan, startled out of the move, took an extra step. The referees, good as they were all game, spotted it. Traveling. There were 5.4 seconds left.

During the time-out, the kids knew the play I'd call. Who didn't? We knew Duke would foul. We wanted the ball in either Rip or Khalid's hands. We put Albert in, a good foul shooter. Ricky is solid. We weren't afraid even if Kevin had to take the shots. He has a way of willing the ball into the basket when we need the points. We decided that after the foul shots, no matter how many were made, we weren't going to call a time-out. We didn't want Duke to be able to run some end-of-the-game set play.

Khalid received the ball and was fouled. We thought this was perfect. No doubt the rest of the world saw a 19-year-old kid who was 5 for 12 from the floor, 0 for 2 from the line. We saw our man at the edge, the lover of the spotlight, winning time. He stepped away from the line. He bobbled the ball. He elaborately practiced his stroke. He made the first. He made the second.

The second shot gave us a three-point lead, that fine cushion. The worst that could happen would be a Duke heave that tied the game and forced an overtime. We sent Rashamel in for Albert. Duke didn't call time-out.

Trajan got the pass and dribbled up the floor . . .

Rash stayed with him . . .

Trajan slipped . . .

Rash had the ball . . .

I had come up the sideline as the play unfolded. I was past center court. I could hear Dave and Karl and Tom yelling, "Coach . . . coach . . ." If you look at the films, it's as if I'm helping to guard Trajan back up the floor, coming along with the action. When Rash got the ball, crazy, the thought came into my mind: *Tate George.* I remembered when Tate had the ball in that Laettner game and bobbled it out of bounds, setting the stage for Laettner. The thought stayed for a second, two seconds, whatever it was.

Rash threw the ball into the air.

The game was over.

             •   ◦   •

I don't think I understood what happened. Again, if you look at the tapes, you will see that there is no expression on my face. This was nothing at all like Gonzaga. Dave grabbed me. I shook Mike's hand and we talked about the game. I saw Tim Tolokan, who was crying. I hadn't seen him crying since his father's funeral. I did nothing. I didn't cry. I didn't smile. Nothing.

I think I still was playing the game in my head. I probably was going to turn around and say to my coaches, "Are you sure Jake has four fouls?" I probably was trying to figure out whom we'd play next, what the next stop was in the brackets. Okay, we won here; now where do we play next week? Is everybody healthy? What time should we have practice tomorrow? Should I run 'em hard? Or should I loosen the grip? What? I had no emotion. Nothing.

For the 48 hours since Ohio State—maybe for my entire adult life, come to think of it—I had been focused on this game. I couldn't get out of the focus. People were running around, flying all over the place, and I had no idea what to do. I exchanged a couple of hugs, because that was what you were supposed to do, but I don't remember whom I hugged or what I said. I had a blank, blank stare. I had no sense of the magnitude of what happened.

I don't know how long this time fragment lasted. It could have been five minutes, could have been two or three. I have no idea. I was out of it.

I think the way the game ended, in doubt to the end, kept my motor running. There wasn't ever that moment where the result is assured, when everyone starts to give handshakes and smiles on the bench. There was no time for decompression. I know Jimmy Valvano went wild at the end of his game, decided by Lorenzo Charles's put-back at the buzzer, but that was different. That was a shock, a miracle. Jimmy V. probably hadn't even seen the basket, just the air ball that preceded it. This was a grind to the end.

Tate George. I was thinking about Tate George when the buzzer sounded, still nervous about what would happen next.

I truly was a stranger in the middle of the pandemonium. It wasn't until I saw Dave again, however much time had passed, that it all finally hit.

"Holy shit," I said as I hugged him. "We won the national championship." And we had.

*   *   *

I left the final string on the rim for Joe McGinn when I finished the job of cutting down the net. That brought a lot of publicity. I have no idea why I did it. The idea came to me at the moment. It was stupid, probably, I mean, how long was it going to stay there? Some workman probably cleared it away in the next hour. The idea just came to me, though, and it seemed right. It still does. Thanks, Joe.

I went on CBS for the postgame show. I did the press conference, probably talked to 1,200 reporters. I had some touching moments with Pat, with my sons—the people who'd been with me for the entire ride, from Old Lyme High School to St. Petersburg. (Emily didn't come to the game. She was back in the room with her mother. It was a school night.) I saw a bunch of those people who were sitting in those 96 family seats. I saw Dee Rowe, sort of the spirit of UConn basketball, a great guy who coached here for eight years and has been an assistant athletic director for 20.

"You've just made me about 100 times smarter than I ever was," he said. "I tell people, 'Yeah, I was once the basketball coach at UConn.' And it means something entirely different."

The locker room was wonderful. There is a picture someone took that is my favorite picture of all time. It's a little out of focus and the lighting isn't great, but it tells the entire story. It's a team picture, the inside, the core of what we are. I'm in it, all the coaches are in it. Lew Perkins is in it. Joe Sharpe. Ted Taigen. Josh, the manager. All of the players are in it, including our redshirts, Ajou Ajou Deng and Justin Brown and Beau

Archibald, and our walk-ons, Ed Tonella and Richard Moore. And that's it. No one else.

Everybody in that picture is someone I've yelled at, screamed at. I've said to each of these kids, "I don't know if you can play for us." I've said, "If you want to score a basket for us, first you're going to have to prove to me that you can score a basket." I've said, "I don't know if you can come back off this injury if you don't work a little harder." I have said . . . there are things perhaps you don't want to know that I've said. The group is the unit that matters. All of us, together, have shared the small passions and fist-fights of everyday life.

And all of us are smiling.

How do you get a picture like that? Every single person has this huge, shit-eating grin. You couldn't pose people that way. A couple of people wouldn't react, wouldn't say cheese at the right time. No, a picture like this has to come from inside. Everyone is just so happy, and it shows. This is the fruition of all that work, the joy of accomplishment.

All of us are smiling.

That's the great thing about sports, isn't it? You get in a picture like that and 50-year-old men, all of us, everyone, we're just a bunch of happy college freshmen for the moment.

＊　　＊　　＊

The game was so late, followed by all of the postgame business, that it wasn't until after two when we arrived back at the Hyatt Regency Westshore. We had the motorcycle escort, the whole show. There must have been 1,500 people waiting for us, UConn people, everyone we ever had known. The band was there.

When you win the national championship, you win a second trophy, the Sears Trophy, made out of Waterford crystal, at the same time. The presentation wasn't supposed to take place until the next day, but I told Lew Perkins we should do it right there in the lobby.

"The people here deserve something," I said.

"Well, we could just present it again tomorrow," Lew said.

It was a terrific celebration. The kids had no curfew, but I did tell them they already had made a big headline for tomorrow and they didn't have to make another one—understand? Most of them went off with their friends. I got to see a bunch of the people I hadn't been able to see all week.

"This is just so great," Bob Samuelson said, crying, recovering from his bypass surgery, lying on a couch in the lobby. "But I'm soooo tired."

"Me too," I said.

It was five o'clock in the morning by the time Pat and I reached our room. We had to get up at seven. For a while the national championship trophy had been missing, but Josh had stored it in his room for safekeeping. I had it now. I put it at the foot of the bed.

Alone with Pat, we talked about the celebration at the Milton-Dedham line when two police cruisers greeted the team bus after we won the Bay State League championship. We talked about driving to scout games in Pittsburgh. Did you ever drive from Boston to Pittsburgh? Don't. We talked about having only $40 in our pocket and being stopped for a $50 speeding ticket. We talked about the time her parents came to visit in Old Lyme and we took them to Gillette Castle, a tourist attraction, and we had only enough money to pay for the two of them and one of us to take the tour. (I went. Pat stayed with Jim junior.) We talked. . . .

This was her triumph as much as mine. She has been a partner in all my crimes and misdemeanors, my sounding board, my absolute best friend as well as the mother to my children. She has spent half her lifetime in gymnasiums, the rest of the crowd gone, waiting for me as I continued to yip and yap about some three-second call that none of the three officials somehow could see. She has endured the long hours and separations that have strangled a bunch of marriages in my profession.

An annoying thing happens when a man gains a measure of success. His partner becomes introduced solely as his partner. ("Say hello to Jim Calhoun's wife.") People mean well, but I hate that. Pat Calhoun certainly always has been her own person, witty and intelligent and pleasant, the best person I know. I don't know where I'd be if I'd never met her. She has been a huge part of the entire ride.

"We did it," I said.

"We did it," she said.

I looked at the trophy at the foot of the bed and had the wacky worry that if I slept this was going to be like *Groundhog Day,* the movie, where I would wake up and discover that I had to go through the whole day again. I slept for two hours. I opened my eyes and looked to the foot of the bed.

The trophy was exactly where I'd left it.

I felt great.

.   .   .

The CBS broadcast of the game was replayed on the plane ride home. The kids loved that. They always love to watch themselves on television. I think they might have even liked this more than *Goodfellas.*

We landed at Bradley Airport—"UConn 1" was the tower's designation for our plane—and then we took a ride back to campus that never will be repeated, not if the University of Connecticut wins 100 of these trophies.

The Beatles did not have a better reception when they came to America. There was a crowd at the airport when we arrived in the middle of the afternoon. There was a crowd as we left the airport. There was a crowd for that entire 30-mile—15 minutes by Howie Dickenman's driving—trip to Storrs.

How can there be a crowd along an interstate? There just was. Cars were parked along the side of the highway. Fire engines were parked at exits, the ladders extended with "UConn #1" signs on the tops. People waved from the bridges. People honked horns from passing cars. People stood on the roof of Gerber Industries.

The ride down route 195 to the campus was filled with people. Waving. Bowing, as if a king were passing. People popped up through their sunroofs on the highway, 65 miles an hour, waving, raising one finger to the sky, doing *something*. Everything was spontaneous, from the heart, real. At Gampel Pavilion, every seat was filled for a welcome-home rally. A crowd—I don't know, 4,000, 5,000 people—hung around outside—as we went through the doors.

Every player was introduced. Every coach.

I came on last.

"Nine years ago, we came back here and you mended our broken hearts," I said. "Well, yesterday we broke some hearts and kicked some ass."

I shouldn't have said that. I really shouldn't. There have been offers since then to put that quote on T-shirts and hats and bumper stickers. I don't want anything to do with that. In the sport we play, in the college environment we live, it was totally inappropriate. It is inappropriate to speak of a respected opponent like that.

And yet . . .

At the moment?

I don't think there ever could have been a more appropriate comment. I don't regret it one bit.

Chapter 10

STORRS

Dear Jim,

Once again, congratulations to you and your team for the national championship. You did a magnificent job of preparing your team for the championship game and your players executed your plan as near to perfection as you could expect....

John Wooden
Westwood, CA

———————————

Jim,

Congratulations. That was one of the greatest coaching jobs I have seen in a long time. You really deserved to win, and it is something you'll never forget.

Red Auerbach
Washington, D.C.

The next couple of months after St. Petersburg were a blur. Do you know that call my doctor gets every year when I say I feel sick and he checks the records and says the basketball season must have just ended because I'm depressed again? There was no call this year. There was no time to be depressed.

I had no idea what happens when you win a national championship. If I did, I probably would have been too nervous before the final game ever to win it. No kidding. The national championship, it seems, puts you on America's A-list. In that brief afterglow of achievement, you become a wanted figure for the cocktail parties and panel discussions of modern life.

Opportunites arrive that you never knew existed.

Invitations come from famous addresses.

It all keeps you pretty busy.

* * *

The President, Bill Clinton, called on Wednesday after the game. Tim Tolokan recorded our conversation for future historians and scholars. The President was in the midst of all that nasty business with NATO and Kosovo.

President: Hello?

Me: President Clinton.

President: Coach, congratulations. How are you doing?

Me: Good. How are you doing? I know you have a lot of things on your mind, and I really appreciate your calling.

President: Well, I apologize I haven't called earlier . . . I had a bunch of people over [at the White House], probably 50 people, to watch the game, and I don't know if I've ever seen a better championship, including the one my home-state team won five years ago. It was magnificent, and it was no fluke. And the thing I liked the best was what Mike Krzyzewski said after it was over. He said, 'We didn't lose this game tonight, we were defeated.' . . . It was the kind of thing college athletics ought to be all about. . . .

I just want to congratulate you. I was thrilled. It was exhilarating. It was a great break for me, and I really enjoyed it. . . . We look forward to seeing you and your team down here. We'll set it up and we'll see you soon, I hope.

Me: Thanks, Bill.

President: Bye-bye, Jim.

Me: Bye-bye.

Notice that I called the president of the United States Bill. Notice also that the president of the United States called me Jim.

That was just the beginning.

.   .   .

Name a fantasy and there is a pretty good chance that in the two months after St. Petersburg, I did it:

• I was invited to go to the final day of the Masters at Augusta National. I was invited, the day after the Masters, to play the same 18 holes at Augusta, the pin placements the same as when José-Maria Olazabal won the tournament a day earlier. I shot 81, no lie, no mulligans, made it through Amen Corner in a breeze. I still wouldn't have made the cut. I checked.

• I threw out the first ball at Fenway Park. Jimmy called from Oregon and told me to throw low, because that way the catcher could block the ball. If I threw high, it could go right to the backstop. Jeff called from Hartford and asked what kind of shoes I was wearing. "Loafers," I said. He told me to wear sneakers so I wouldn't slip on the mound. I wore sneakers, I threw low, and the ball didn't go to the backstop.

• I went on the David Letterman show, a show I watch every night when there isn't a good Pepperdine–Santa Clara thriller on ESPN at the same time. Steve Martin and Goldie Hawn were the other guests. (Strange— in person, Goldie didn't remind me of my mother.) Dave asked if I ever yelled or swore at my players. I said, "I guess you haven't watched me coach." That got a laugh. At least in Connecticut.

• I went to the White House Correspondents' Dinner, black tie, in Washington. I was a guest of *People* magazine. Bill and I didn't run into each other. We both were busy. That happens sometimes at parties.

• I went to the Wooden Awards in Los Angeles with Rip, who was a finalist for Player of the Year. I sat and talked basketball with John Wooden and Dean Smith. They both had the same secret for basketball success: good players. I was glad to hear my own theory validated.

• I went to the Winged Foot Awards at the New York Athletic Club, where I received the Coach of the Year Award. Donny Marshall, who played on some good UConn teams for me, stood and spoke. He said his high school coach never had yelled at him in the state of Washington. His high school coach had doubled as the music teacher. The coach was a quiet, thoughtful man. Then, Donny said, he went to UConn . . . that got a laugh. At least from the Connecticut people in the crowd.

• I received an honorary degree at Trinity College. Rita Moreno, the actress, also received one. The other recipients, I did not know. They had done things so complicated and wonderful I couldn't even spell the words that described their accomplishments.

• I gave a speech in Banff, Alberta. The pilot on the plane sent out free champagne and, as we were landing in Calgary, announced that it was "an honor to have Jim Calhoun, coach of the NCAA champion University of Connecticut basketball team, on board." The passengers applauded, as we landed in Calgary, Alberta.

• I gave a speech at the Oakdale Music Circus in Wallingford, Connecticut. It was part of a seminar on success run by Peter Lowe. George and Barbara Bush preceded me. Colin Powell followed me. I had 20 minutes to explain how to be a success. It seemed like a short amount of time.

• I went to a Nike clinic in Las Vegas. I went to a Nike clinic in Minneapolis. I played in a CBS charity golf tournament in Florida. I went to a banquet at Northeastern. I went to a banquet in Braintree. I was invited to throw out the first pitch at Yankee Stadium. I was invited to throw out the first pitch at Wrigley Field. I . . .

• Did I mention the parade through downtown Hartford, the crowd estimated between 250,000 and 300,000 people. Did I mention that experience, riding in the back of somebody's red Mercedes convertible, Silly String squirted all over me, the kids on the team on a float, waving and signing autographs, everybody being treated like Hollywood stars? Did I mention the visit to the state assembly, the standing ovation? There was a whole lot of other stuff, too.

I lived on a cloud.
I lived on a pink, fluffy cloud.

* * *

A breakup dinner was held at my house on a weekday evening in the midst of all of this. It's an annual event. I like having it at my house, because this is the first place all of these kids visited when they were being recruited. I want them to know from the beginning that we are family, all of us, and I will treat them like family. I think it's nice for the seniors to end their time at the house, everything coming full circle.

Rip couldn't attend. He was in Buffalo, already on the move. He had declared himself eligible for the NBA draft, skipping his senior year. It was not big news. The television stations didn't even break into the soap operas for this press conference, the decision was so obvious. It was time for him to go, time for him to make some big money. He's more than ready now. I think he'll be a great pro.

Antric didn't come. He called and said his car broke down. That's

Antric to the end. He's graduated, and I want him to buy a couple of good suits and get a haircut and attack the business world. He's a smart kid and I can see him in a corner office at Aetna Insurance or some other big company someday, pulling down $300,000 a year. I'm afraid, though, he's going to try to play basketball in Europe for small money, no matter what I tell him. That's Antric.

The other kids all showed up. They had been busy, these kids, as busy as I had been. They all had to climb through their final exams after the national championship, a tough thing to do when you're signing autographs everywhere you go. ("Sign my blue book? Please?") I told Ted this was his version of the Final Four. A lot of teams have had big academic problems after winning the NCAAs—I checked—and I didn't want that here. Everyone survived. Ted did nice work.

Ricky, who graduated, had become Connecticut's favorite son. He received more fan mail than anyone. I think people responded to the way he played, to his hard work. It didn't hurt, either, that he made the play that beat Duke. If he stays in the state, he can eat a free lunch every day for the rest of his life. He already is a spokesman for Bob's Stores, getting into the commercial aspect. He can try to make the NBA as a free agent, and certainly he could go to Europe. He has a brother who played football at Clemson, and a couple of pro football teams have inquired about him as a defensive back.

Rash, who also graduated, will probably go to Europe and have a good career. He is a terrific player. I still feel bad for him. He was caught by the situation he was in and never complained. There was a certain justice that he wound up with the ball at the end of the game at the end of it all.

E.J., the fourth graduate, will also be fine. He will get a job, prosper. He always will be a part of this history. An E. J. Harrison Day was held in Danbury. I think that's wonderful. There were days, banquets, celebrations for most of these kids. Albert Mouring Day in little Preston, Maryland— wouldn't you have loved to see that? I don't think there would have been an E. J. Harrison Day if he'd stayed at Western Connecticut, even if he'd scored another 1,000 points. I hope he feels he made the right decision.

Khalid . . . don't get me started. He was on Letterman a couple of nights after I was and a couple of nights after that was picked up in Hartford on marijuana possession. We have had long talks about that, believe me. I think it was a setup, a sting, that he was caught in, but that doesn't get him off the hook. He apologized, publicly and privately, and he was sincere. Life on the edge . . . He's a high-maintainence kid, for sure, you have to pay the full toll with Khalid, but he's worth it. Just seeing him walk down the hall makes me smile. I'm very happy that he decided to stay in school for at least another year. I think he'll be an even better player next year.

Khalid, Kevin, Jake, Albert, Edmund, Souleymane . . . they'll all be back, and I like our chances again in 2000. Ajou, who has become our not-so-secret weapon, could fill a lot of holes in the offense for us. Khalid told reporters all season that Ajou, a redshirt who never plays in public, was the best player on the team. Howie Dickenman tells me not to let Ajou eat too much because if he puts on bulk, he'll only be around for a year before the NBA calls. Ajou could be very good. Justin Brown went back to Australia with orders to bulk up, too. He could move into the picture. Our three recruits—Marcus Cox, Tony Robertson, and Doug Wrenn—each could provide instant help.

You never can be sure about a team, though, about what chemistry is going to evolve, about whether all the parts will fit next to all the other parts, each working in harmony with the others. If it were strictly a talent game, measured by height and weight and scoring averages and vertical rise, well . . . Duke had four players picked in the first 14 selections of the first round of the NBA draft. We had Rip.

I loved our cohesiveness this year. I loved our unselfishness. It is a rare thing to see these days, individual sacrifice for a group goal. What we saw with this team is a rare thing. I loved our composure. No team since Texas Western in 1966, that famous black-white game against Kentucky, had won a national championship on its first trip to the Final Four. That was a statistic staring these kids in the face. That was a stat they overcame.

No Connecticut team—not next year, not in any year, no matter how good it might be—can do what this Connecticut team did. These kids did it first.

I don't think we'll have any breakup dinner where the breakup will be harder.

.   .   .

The pace has slowed a little bit now. I asked Pat the other day if there was any mail, and she said there was only the gas bill and a letter from Publishers Clearing House announcing that I might have won a couple million dollars. So I guess we're getting there, a little closer to normal.

I still am amazed, really, at what this championship has meant to so many people. I still am amazed at the significance it seemed to have in so many lives around the state. I still hear stories every day. *Where were you when UConn won the NCAAs?* I think that will be a marker for people in Connecticut for years to come.

I use the phrase "It's not a Polaroid, it's a movie" when I try to describe what happened here. The Polaroid is this moment, the celebration that started when Rash threw the ball into the air, the parades and dinners, the phone call from my friend Bill. The Polaroid is very nice—wonderful, really—but the movie is what really happened, what counted most. The perseverance. The slow climb. I think that is what the people in the state understand, why this is meaningful.

I wouldn't, really, have changed a thing.

The Purdue University Boilermakers won the women's NCAA championship this year. They were coached by a 33-year-old woman, Carolyn Peck, in her first year as a head coach. That's quite an achievement, for sure, but you know what? I like my longer trip better.

I like the way those grown-up kids from Old Lyme and Dedham and Steve DeCosta from Westport feel they are a part of this. I like the dignity that somehow extends now to those forgotten Northeastern teams, teams that deserved more than they received when they did some wonderful things and not many people noticed. Reggie Lewis, bless his soul, was a part of this national championship. Yes, he was.

I don't mind Christian Laettner's shot anymore. I really don't. I'm glad that he made it.

I don't mind the sad finish at the foul line in Florida, Donyell's two misses. Donyell has been fine. We've all been fine.

I don't mind the tough brackets that we drew, UCLA in California, North Carolina in North Carolina.

I don't even mind the yapping and yipping of the Horde. That has only added to the meaning at the end, the "Yes, UConn" and "King Conn" and "Conn You Believe It?" headlines.

There have been no back doors opened to make all this happen. There have been no secret deals, no special privileges. There is something to be said about starting out in a Plymouth Duster or, yes, a Dodge Shitbox and winding up in a red Mercedes, even someone else's red Mercedes, as people shout your name.

Maybe it's that old New England Puritan ethic. (I do like the Red Sox, remember.) Suffering is good. Pain forms character. Work will get you to the Promised Land eventually, if you just keep kicking. To win the national championship at 33, to me, would be too easy. I like the way it all has played out here.

The future?

Who knows?

I don't know how long I'm going to continue doing this, throwing myself into this 24-hour-a-day, 365-day-a-year job. I've always said I don't want to become that old coach who confuses the names of today's players with the names of yesterday's players, running on past successes. I think I'm a ways from that. I still remember the names. I remember the names all too well. I think about today's players all the time, around the clock—about ways they can improve, about ways we can improve, about how we're going to handle this monster schedule in the new season, about whether Jake's foot will be better, about Soule's offense, about whether Albert can step up, about whether Kevin is happy, about the new kids, about what the schedule, the routine, and maybe the menu for dinner should be tomorrow.

I'm not done yet.

* * *

My son Jim is the entrepreneur in the family. His mother called him "our Alex Keaton" when he was young, comparing him to the Republican-loving, ultracapitalist teenager Michael J. Fox played in *Family Ties*. Jim always has grand ideas about Storrs. We talk about them all the time. Here's where we'll build the mall. There's where we'll build the hotel. The movie theater? Maybe over near the horse barns.

None of this happens, of course. It's our little joke. Storrs is Storrs.

It is what it is—in the middle of nowhere.

A kid, a potential player, came to visit during the Memorial Day weekend. He was a good player from Massachusetts who played a year for North Carolina State and now wanted to transfer. He was looking at half a dozen schools. He arrived with his mother.

I took them for the grand tour of the campus. Classes were finished for the semester. Summer school hadn't begun. Because of the holiday, all of the workers were home. Not a single person was walking along the side-walks, lounging in the student union, even lining up for ice cream. The landscape was something from a science-fiction movie.

"Is there a place we can get something to eat on the way home?" the mother asked when we got back to the office.

"Not much around here is open today," Dave said. "Rein's Delicatessen is very good."

Rein's Delicatessen is about 15 miles from campus. Geez.

I looked around me.

National champions. How did the whole thing ever happen? How did we ever get from where we were to where we are? The NCAA trophy was on a table in my office. In 13 seasons, all we ever wanted to do, starting at ground zero, had been accomplished. All the long nights had paid off. All the trips to all the homes all over the country had paid off. All the building, one year after another, had paid off. Here—this small place in the corner of this small state—was the capitol of college basketball. Here.

This is it? I could hear the kid, the potential transfer, saying in his mind. *This is it?*

A few weeks later he enrolled in Auburn.

I guess he just didn't have the right imagination to be a champion.

Acknowledgments

It all began with my mother and my father in my hometown of Braintree, Massachusetts. I have always felt their love and am grateful for their guidance. Thank you to everyone in Braintree, especially my coach and mentor, Fred Herget.

I spent 14 wonderful years at Northeastern University and will always have fond memories of times spent with colleagues and friends. I'll remember Bunny Solomon, my Northeastern rabbi, for his guidance; Jack Grinold, a friend who really cared; and Dr. Keith Motley, my first recruit and a very special person.

The past 13 years at the University of Connecticut has brought me in close contact with a number of special people who have provided me with encouragement, advice, and enthusiastic support. They include: former Director of Athletics John Toner, who dared to dream about Jim Calhoun in the spring of 1986; current Director of Athletics Lew Perkins and Senior Associate Director of Athletics Jeff Hathaway, who steer the ship that is the UConn Division of Athletics in such a first-class fashion; former UConn basketball head coach Donald "Dee" Rowe, whom I respect greatly as a basketball man and as a personal counsel; former UConn President Dr. Harry Hartley, my long-time jogging partner; and our third man in the ring, Dr. George Drumm; Nick Buonocore, a UConn basketball junkie and friend from the Sugar Shack; Bob Samuels, a dear friend and supporter who introduced me to a very meaningful relationship with the Juvenile Diabetes Foundation.

Both on the court, and in those rare moments away from the game, I've been blessed with a special group of friends who truly care. Gerry and Ellen Roisman, who befriended the Calhoun family when we arrived in Connecticut and have remained a positive constant through the years. Peter and Emily Roisman; Peter is my agent, both are our friends. Bob and Nancy Samuelson, whose friendship we have treasured for more than 35 years, a friendship that as each year passes grows more special. Tim and Diane Tolokan, our first and best friends at UConn, a part of our family, and two of the most caring people we know. Jim and Pat Raynor—Jim's my dentist and workout partner, Pat's my conscience. Both are our friends. Bernie and Beth Schilberg, wonderful friends who light up our lives with their caring support. Kevin and Betsy Tubridy, our designer, our neighbors, and amazingly still our friends. Lew and Gwen Perkins—he's my boss, they're our friends. Herb and Marcia Dunn, two of the biggest UConn fans and our friends.

I offer sincere thanks to colleagues who helped make this book a reality. The idea took flight through the efforts of literary agent Esther Newberg, who provided the guidance and skill from the very beginning of the project, and Luke Dempsey, who believed in the book from day one. Again, to Tim Tolokan, who for 13 years has been the best publicist for UConn basketball. I am grateful for all his hours of labor, insightful and untiring research, and most of all for his support and friendship.

To Leigh Montville, my collaborator and assistant coach on this book. Leigh is a gifted writer and UConn alum. We spent many hours talking and sharing ideas, not only about the game of basketball but also the game of life. It is because of him that I feel the book captures the essence of this championship season. Leigh has my enduring thanks and friendship.

My basketball assistant coaches through the years have played a major role in insuring our success through their tireless and extraordinary efforts. They include: Dave Leitao, Karl Hobbs, Tom Moore, Howie Dickenmann, Glen Miller, Steve Pikiell, Ted Woodward, Scott Wissel, Bill Cardarelli, Karl Fogel, Keith Motley, and Kevin Stacom.

Connecticut basketball is a total program because our support staff is the best. Dr. Ted Taigen is our academic MVP and serves as the godfather to our players while also standing tall as my colleague and friend. Joe

Sharpe is America's greatest trainer who has become an extended member of the Calhoun family. Amy Wamester is my administrative assistant who handles all details with intelligence, grace, and spirit. And Linda White-house, who has been with us from the start. They are our center and make our daily lives so much easier.

Pat's family, which is my second family, has always been there as supporters of our efforts—both at Northeastern and at Connecticut. Pat's brother Larry McDevitt; Pat's sister Marie McDevitt; Pat's sister Eileen Fucile and her husband, Bob; Pat's brother Jim McDevitt and his wife, Dot McCann; Pat's sister Chris McDevitt and her husband, Darrel Galles; Pat's sister Nanci Sheppard and her husband, Gerry; my nephew Mike Haglof, who has become my third son; and lastly a very special lady, Pat's mother and my other mom, Mary McDevitt.

I've always known that my sisters and brother and their families were there to cheer us to victory and to quietly support and encourage me when we faced defeat. My sister Rose, who helped me through everything along the way more than she'll ever know. My sister Margaret, the quite one who keeps making sure I remember I'm from Braintree. My sister Kathy, who kept us all organized and moving forward. My sister Joan, who makes me laugh like my mother did and serves the role of family host. My brother Bill, whom I've been a father to, a brother of, and now I've become his biggest fan. Joining my siblings as loyal supporters are their spouses. Rose's husband, Manny Dias; Margaret's husband, Jim McKeough; Kathy's husband, Richard Eaton; Joan's husband, Steve Girard; and Bill's wife, Sheela.

In addition to the above mentioned family members, I must add a very vocal cheering section, my many nieces and nephews.

Other special people who deserve mention are: Joe and Sheila McGinn, Mother Shawn and all of our supporters at the Franciscan Life Center, Joyce Leitao, Joanne Hobbs, Eileen Moore, Jan Taigen, Dave Kaplan, Josh Nochimson, Alyssa Budkofsky, Lawrence Morello, Dave Gavitt, Tom and Cheryl Cannon, Tom and Carol Kerr, Jim Davis, Neal Kearney, Carl Martin, Hope Angelone, Cathy Davis, Bill Mitchell, Brian Smith, Ron Dubois, and Marley.

This book, like everything else I'll ever do, is directly linked to my biggest fans, my immediate family. My granddaughter Emily, the only undefeated Calhoun. My daughter-in-law Jen, and my future daughter-in-law Amy, the best recruits on the Calhoun team. My sons, Jim and Jeff, the two true stars in their father's life. My wife Pat, my best friend and lifetime recruit.

Printed in the United States
by Baker & Taylor Publisher Services